'I'm not going to

movie he has made today. It's just unbelievable what the women in India are capable of doing. Today, nobody is talking about Pallavi ji's acting or any of the actors that did a phenomenal performance because we were just engrossed [in the movie] and we want to know the end. Who are these scientists who saved us literally? We have an extraordinary storyteller … to tell a story and engross us in a storytelling [that] is so powerful that we forget all our differences and see the movie. And when that is combined with a deep sense of patriotism, a deep sense of humanity, then that becomes a potent weapon, and the result of that potent weapon changes the entire world in a day. I was so moved and so teary as all of us were today. Vivek, that is your biggest victory.'

**R. Madhavan**, actor and director

'It was a story of triumph, of overcoming obstacles, during the very tragic time in history, where you have a people that were struggling – not just in India but all over the world people were dying. People were scared, people were depressed, people needed help. This is an inspired movie, not just about doctors, not just about scientists, not just about women, not just about any [but] it's a human triumph over despair and tragedy, and I think it was something we need, something to remind us that we come out of something and then we can continue to dominate. When people are losing hope, it takes just one person to say, yes, we can; yes, we are worthy; yes, this fight is worth fighting. We are not going to accept defeat, we are not going to accept resignation, we are not going to accept any negativity between us and success. We're going to make huge sacrifices, even if it comes to not spending time with our families. Our time, our sleep – it's worth it. We can actually achieve something so great and give hope for everybody for the future.'

**Dr Rich McCormick**, Congressmen, Georgia, US

'I'm here to support the movie as well as what India has achieved in developing a vaccine, which they have provided to many other countries, including Myanmar, to save humanity. Thank you so much. We are very grateful for your support.'

**Myat Nyi Nyi Win**, Deputy Chief of Mission, Myanmar

'It's really heart touching, and I do understand the role of women … because she is a mother … a wife and … a career person. It's really hard to balance. My own experience, you know, your family and your work, but some people – fortunately in my case my parents were downstairs, and I was upstairs, so I could do better – and all these women did not have that. It is not easy for a woman with children to have a career. She requires a really good family support. I always say that behind every successful woman there's an understanding man, otherwise she can't do it, including Pallavi Joshi. You really require a very understanding husband, and in this film the children were small, but they will be proud of their mothers, what she has done, and for the common man, we know they won't understand what is Covaxin, but this movie clearly shows the effort, the kind you know it's not just work; it's a selfless work all these scientists did so that they spent their maximum time in this in that period, so that we all can live in a democratic India happily and healthy. That's a very important message…. I always have a discussion with Mohandas bhai [that] thousands of years we have been slave, so we have lost our identity, our courage, our capacity. We have tremendous potential, and we are not unleashing it because we are always worried [that] we will not be able to do it. Many people say we can't do it … [but] we can … we should believe in ourselves. The beauty is not in the dress or the money or the make up or what – it's nothing [like] that. The beauty of a person is in the courage or in the confidence…. There's a very famous sloka in Sanskritam: In general, it is not the dress; if you have vishwas in you, that's the real beauty, and that's the real honesty and that's the real money. And that you have shown here – that the real wealth is in our confidence. Please unleash your potential. All Indians, be ethical, hard working and be proud that you are Indian.'

**Sudha Murty**, educator, philanthropist and author

'We are highly inspired by this movie. Every five to seven minutes, I had tears rolling out of my eyes. That's the power and impact it has.'

**Swami Mitrananda ji**, mentor and head of Chinmaya Mission, Chennai

'Absolutely fantastic and beautiful movie, bringing out the very essence of the spirit of Bharat, especially the women of Bharat. I Congratulate you and wish you the best, and may India be proud of all our achievement. *Bharat Mata ki jai*.'

**Swami Swaroopananda ji**, global head of Chinmaya Mission

'Our scientists have done tremendous work, and they need all the congratulations in the world for the wonderful work they did to help people throughout the world not just in India. Many countries have benefited your work and your dedication, and I understand from Vivek ji that many women are engaged in this – *nari shakti*; *bohot acha kaam kiya. Aap sabko bohot bohot badhai, bohot bohot ashirvad*.'

**Sri Sri Ravishankar**, yoga guru and spiritual leader

'The role models of our country need to be changed. Scientists have to be our role model. How inspiring it is to see women scientists – what they are doing for the country. It inspired a lot of people to join the right profession where you can make a great difference. Stories like this have to come out. And I feel it is a very difficult film in the way the wonderful moments it has created. I told them that *The Tashkent Files* was a very difficult film. This was even more difficult. They have, with heart and soul, put it forward. I wish them all the best.'

**Prasoon Joshi**, writer, poet, lyricist and advertising guru

*'Film toh bohot hi sundar hai; bohot hi anand aaya dekh ke. Aur ICMR aur NIV ka bohot hi hridey ki geheraiyon se aabahar. Agar inke personal sacrifice nahi hote toh Bharat me karodo log vaccine ke bina kaise hi guzara karte. Bohot bohot dhanyavad. Aur doosra Vivek Agnihotri ji aur unki poori team ka main bohot hi abhinandan karna chahungi. Inhone mahila samaan ke liye yeh ek film banai. Apki star cast bohot hi impeccable thi. Aapko bohot shubhkaamnaye, aur Bharat mata ki jaye.'*

**Nupur Sharma**, national spokesperson, BJP

# Testimonies of Real-Life Characters

'The Covid-19 pandemic caused much misery, sufferings and death across the world. Several countries braved and faced the pandemic. India, a rich civilisation, faced the pandemic with tremendous courage and determination unitedly, and demonstrated to the world that every individual has a role as a world citizen: Vasudhaiv Kutumbkam: The world is one family.

Around the world, doctors, nurses, scientists and frontline workers risked their own lives to help save others. This new virus had no known treatments, and it was imperative to develop a vaccine to save humanity. The hard work of the scientists of India helped develop a vaccine in record time under testing circumstances. The majority of the scientists who were in this team were women. These women with immense capabilities worked tirelessly to develop the Indian vaccine, which was rapidly deployed not only across India but to more than a hundred countries across the world.

The film *The Vaccine War* has very cinematically shown this true story to the world. It has clearly shown how the ingenious Indian women have been at the forefront of this triumph. This commendable feat is an extraordinary achievement, which motivates not only the current generation but will continue to inspire generations to come. The maverick geniuses of all involved in the depiction of this true story deserve accolades and acclaim worldwide.'

**Prof. Balram Bhargava** is the former director general of Indian Council of Medical Research.
He is the current chief of the Cardiothoracic and Neurosciences Centre, All India Institute of Medical Science, New Delhi

'This movie portrays a lot of the challenges, pressures and chaos that the pandemic caused in our country. However, even during the chaos, ICMR and NIV took on the challenge of screening patients with respiratory symptoms, especially those returning to India from overseas. Scientists at ICMR-NIV not only confirmed the first cases in the country but also went on to view the virus under the electron microscope and even isolate (grow) the virus, becoming the fifth country in the world to do so.

There were many challenging projects that were undertaken: sending NIV scientists to Iran to screen stranded Indian nationals there to facilitate their repatriation; strengthening more than 3,000 labs across the country by sending reagents to them; studying anti-viral activity in many compounds that were sent to NIV; training personnel from other labs; establishing antibody screening tests for the COVID-19 virus, etc. (much of the latter could not obviously be all portrayed in the movie).

Of course, the most important venture was working with industry to make an indigenous vaccine for India. The movie portrays the difficulties in procuring the animals, particularly the monkeys, and the challenges and rigour of doing those elaborate experiments in animals. These pre-clinical trials were vital to complete before the vaccine could gain approval for clinical trials. The race against time and the personal stress it caused to the scientists and other staff come through clearly in the movie.

This movie is an extraordinary saga of amazing teamwork. Despite the stress and pressure of work at that time, Indian scientists did a commendable job in the thick of this pandemic.'

**Dr Priya Abraham**, former director,
National Institute of Virology, Pune.
Currently she is a professor of clinical virology at CMC Vellore.

'The COVID-19 pandemic was a public health emergency of a magnitude that was never ever witnessed by mankind. Due to various reasons, India became a cause of global concern and was viewed as a potential epicentre of possibly the worst spurt of COVID-19 cases, thus posing a threat to the entire world. In March 2020, the country had less than 300 COVID-19 testing laboratories, severe dearth of testing kits and personal protective equipment (PPE), no plan of vaccine development and ill-prepared healthcare settings with poor infrastructure and untrained staff. Overall, India's preparedness to fight the pandemic of this scale was sub-optimal. However, against all these gigantic challenges, in March 2020, amidst immense global pressure, the Indian government, scientists, public health experts, healthcare workers, academia and industry launched their pragmatic fight against the raging pandemic, notably with little understanding of pathophysiology and transmission dynamics, and no artillery of drugs and vaccines. Since then, the country has made colossal strides in augmenting its healthcare infrastructure, laboratory testing network, medical diagnostic industry, PPE production industry, medical oxygen producing capacity and vaccine manufacturing capacity as well as its roll-out. The achievements made by India within a short timespan after the emergence of COVID-19 pandemic in 2020 have strengthened the country tremendously and have huge future implications as well.

There are several unsung heroes, untold stories and immense sacrifices of all cadres of professionals across various sectors, which enabled India to adequately equip itself to fight back the pandemic. Amongst other, one of the major challenges posed was the development of a safe, effective and affordable vaccine for one of the most populous countries of the world, and once developed, vaccinate every eligible individual. The country's leadership decided to adopt a bi-pronged strategy for vaccine development. The first approach was to initiate indigenous R&D for de-novo vaccine development, mainly to prove the scientific prowess of India to the world. This resulted in the development of Covaxin. The second approach involved technology transfer of effective, feasible and affordable vaccines available across the world and quickly scale up production after doing short bridging trials in the Indian population. One of the major success stories of this effort is the development of Covishield. The vaccine industry has been one of India's greatest assets. India supplies 60 per cent of the vaccines globally, and it is not an exaggeration to say that every second child in the world receives vaccines made in India. Usually, successful vaccine development is a 10–15-year pathway, wherein preclinical and clinical studies are conducted sequentially. However, the pandemic created a vital need for expedited approaches and facilitatory regulatory frameworks all over the world. Innovative designs were instituted by researchers and industry. Additionally, preclinical and clinical development pathways were run concurrently and not sequentially, thereby reducing the timeline to about 10 months. Indian academia and industry also implemented these innovative vaccine designs.

Two of the global frontrunners, Covaxin and the Oxford vaccine, Covishield, by Serum Institute of India (SII), are manufactured in India. Covaxin is a completely made-in-India vaccine developed under successful public-private partnership of the ICMR and BBIL, showcasing the skills of atmanirbhar Bharat (self-reliant India). Adult immunisation with the two indigenous vaccines was initiated in India on 16 January 2021 under restricted emergency use authorisation. Overall, India's response to the COVID-19 pandemic is laudable and noteworthy.

I am happy to note that the movie *The Vaccine War* has very realistically portrayed the struggles, challenges and eventual victory of Indian scientists in developing the COVID-19 vaccine in times of utmost crisis.

I congratulate Mr Vivek Agnihotri, the director, and Mrs Pallavi Joshi, the producer of the film, for the precise technical detailing of the film with utmost scientific vigour. The movie has simplified the complex and challenging task of vaccine R&D for common masses. I feel that every Indian, particularly the young minds, must watch the movie, not for the sole purpose of knowing the unsung heroes and their challenges, but more importantly to get motivated and inspired in their own lives. The movie beautifully depicts how unsurmountable challenges can be overcome in the most difficult and resource-limited times. The only requirement to accomplish a determined task is one's own willpower, which makes impossible possible. The movie also depicts the grit, determination and commitment of women in science and demonstrates how one visionary and able leader can change the world. Besides, the movie also exemplifies the value of teamwork and synergy.

*The Vaccine War* is a flawless depiction of India's journey from crisis to opportunity to success, and how due to India's committed workforce and leadership, the country is inching towards its goal of being atmanirbhar (self-reliant). The film gives us accurate glimpses of our collective efforts, innovations and achievements during the worst-ever witnessed humanitarian crisis. I wish all success to the film and urge every Indian to watch it and feel proud of being a Bhartiya.'

**Dr Nivedita Gupta**, senior scientist and head,
Division of Communicable Diseases,
Indian Council of Medical Research, New Delhi

'Movies are one of the most popular kinds of art among the general audience. Indian movie has shown the world the nation's rich cultural diversity and customs. However, science-fiction films are uncommon in the country. The film *The Vaccine War* is based on the true story of Indian scientists who fought COVID-19 by developing a cost-effective vaccine for India and the rest of the world. "We can fight this war with science" was the mantra for hard work of all the scientists whose stories are being told through this movie.

Based on the book *Going Viral* by Prof. Balram Bhargava, former director general, Indian Council of Medical Research, and under the directorial of Mr Vivek Ranjan Agnihotri, this movie is an attempt to shift the spotlight away from sceptics and focus on unsung heroes, frontline workers and determined scientists who worked tirelessly for months to develop India's indigenous COVID-19 vaccine, Covaxin, in collaboration with Bharat Biotech, Hyderabad, and presented one of the fastest public-private partnership success stories. The main benefit of being India's 'first bioscience film', which was released in multiple languages, is that it provided an ease in reaching the common man and giving a message on the role of vaccines in dealing with the COVID-19 pandemic.

The film illustrates our country's real-life problems in managing a pandemic from the ground up, led by the ICMR, one of the country's oldest medical research institutes. Making a film about a scientific subject was challenging, considering the containment facilities that need to be shown in the movie. From isolating the virus and testing the vaccine on mouse models, hamsters and non-human primates to human testing in clinical trials and obtaining approvals for use not only in India but also in other countries, the first-of-its-kind bioscience film is a fitting homage to India's scientists and their perseverance and prowess in developing an indigenous solution in record time amidst numerous personal, political and local challenges. The ICMR-NIV team was blown away by the excellent storyline and narration, which kept the audience engaged throughout.

The film tells the story of the scientists and team of ICMR, who felt that India, too, could develop its vaccine with indigenous capacity in a very short time by following international and national regulatory procedures. The development of Covaxin during the COVID-19 crisis demonstrates the capacity of and partnership between Bharat Biotech and ICMR-NIV Pune. The film captures human emotions clearly, such as the exhilaration over a breakthrough, the helplessness when findings are delayed, the rage when a senior puts pressure and tears of empathy among fellow scientists who are exhausted after numerous sleepless nights. Teamwork, leadership, compassion and empathy are needed in tough time to deliver the right product as well.

Virology is a lesser-known field among the general public, and the film conveys to the audience the significance of this profession. The devotion of the country's researchers and healthcare personnel, who rose to the challenges set by the COVID-19 pandemic, was beautifully depicted. This is also a wake-up call for the country in terms of engraving the "Make in India" concept. The film truly instils trust amongst the general public in Indian research organisations and inspires future generations to pursue a career in biomedical research. This film represents a triumph of an enormous number of government and private professionals working together. The movie emphasises and depicts the ICMR team's hardships and sacrifices as well as how their family members stood beside them during the challenging times and helped them accomplish this incredible task. Though the movie depicted few characters as representative of the story, a large number of unsung heroes worked during the crisis.

I congratulate the filmmakers of *The Vaccine War*, the director, producer, actors and the entire cast and crew, who worked tirelessly to bring our story to the community. The fervour and excitement with which the crew worked on the sets are visible in the film. *The Vaccine War* is a must-watch movie even if for the sole purpose of informing viewers about the hardships, efforts and struggles of the medical and scientific communities, which gave a ray hope to millions by developing the indigenous vaccine.

Overall, *The Vaccine War* fully exemplifies the efforts in developing Covaxin, defining the "atmanirbharta" of atmanirbhar Bharat and demonstrating to the world that "India Can Do It!'"

**Dr Pragya D. Yadav**, M.Sc., PhD, FAMS, FNAASc,
FIVS, MNASc, scientist 'F' and group leader,
Maximum Containment Laboratory, ICMR-NIV Pune

# Movie Reviews

'*The Vaccine War* makes you emotional in certain parts. It would hit you right and make you think about how healthcare professionals and scientists did not care about their lives but gave importance to the greater good. It celebrates their sacrifice and drives home the point without the message being all-too-loud. Watch this film if you want a change from the regular big-screen masala and have an appetite to consume something that is realistic and relevant.'

***India Today***

'*The Vaccine War* is a tale of courage, conviction, and science, as documented in Vivek Agnihotri's follow-up to *The Kashmir Files*. While it can get one-sided in parts, the film does a commendable job of representing the relentless struggles of scientists.'

***Hindustan times***

'Agnihotri gets many things right in making the film an engaging experience for the most part. From creating a sense of dread at the start to generating a mood of urgency and self-belief in the scientific community, the film takes us to the glorious battles fought with majestic microorganisms in laboratories and simultaneously lays out the limitations under which Indian scientists work. The depiction of the ordinary life and sacrifices of the scientists who did extraordinary work during the crisis creates an emotional swell.'

***The Hindu***

'In a triumphant comeback, Nana Patekar shines in *The Vaccine War*. The film, directed by Vivek Agnihotri, tells the remarkable story of India's battle against the virus. It beautifully captures the resilience of scientists and their unwavering dedication.'

**Firstpost**

'The highlighting of the women is the best part of the movie, and its most moving. These are ordinary women, balancing work and home, sometimes with adverse effects on their children. This "Indic feminism", as Agnihotri calls it, is as independent, but more collective and family-oriented than Western feminism.

Agnihotri's movie captures the under-appreciation that follows the careers of most government scientists. The story begins with a virologist's badge being rudely torn from him by the police and being made to sit by the roadside as punishment for breaking lockdown rules. That is a running theme in the film, the lack of recognition, the double burden on the women scientists at home and at work, the scepticism that surrounds their achievements, which are hard to understand for the layperson.'

**Kaveree Bamzai, *Open* magazine**

'*The Vaccine War* is a straightforward underdog story, divided into 12 interconnected chapters that are quite simply fragments of a whole. Based on Balram Bhargava's book *Going Viral*, it tells the story of Covaxin, India's first indigenous and much-scrutinized Covid vaccine, developed on a war footing during the dreary days of pandemic. Fronted by a terrific Nana Patekar, a laborious third act notwithstanding, *The Vaccine War* is an enthralling if wildly aphoristic chronicle of the silent war our scientists waged against an unrelenting enemy.'

**Money Control**

'#*TheVaccineWar* is an important film that *should* be watched by one and all… It's enlightening and inspiring, both… The 'heroes' here are our scientists and #VivekAgnihotri brilliantly showcases their sacrifices and strengths in those 2.40 hours… DON'T MISS IT!'

**Taran Adarsh, film critic, on X (formerly Twitter)**

'Vivek Ranjan Agnihotri's direction is splendid. His narration is engaging, engrossing and entertaining. On the whole, *The Vaccine War* is an outstanding film, which will win both critical acclaim and box-office rewards. It may have started slow, but collections will pick up phenomenally as the hugely positive word of mouth spreads.'

**Komal Nahta, Film Information**

# The Vaccine War

# The Vaccine War

*A True Story*

Vivek Ranjan Agnihotri

ink | OCCAM

**Title:** The Vaccine War: A True Story
**Author:** Vivek Ranjan Agnihotri

**ISBN:** 978-93-92209-74-1

First published in India 2023
This edition published 2023

**Published by:**
BluOne Ink LLP
A-76, 2nd Floor, Sector 136, Noida
Uttar Pradesh 201305

**Website:** www.bluone.ink
**Email:** publisher@bluone.ink



The script has been edited by Manan Agnihotri.

Printed and bound in India at Nutech Print Services

Kali, Occam and BluPrint are all trademarks of BluOne Ink LLP.

ink | OCCAM

1 **EXT. HOSPITAL INTERSECTION – MAGIC HOUR** 1
**April 2020**

The scene opens on a close-up of an earphone on a young cop, who is glued to his mobile phone. A stray dog sits near him. The young cop gives the dog a biscuit. The dog takes a bite and turns to look away into the distance. The young cop follows the dog's perspective.

In the far distance, ambulances are zipping in and out. It seems the world has ended. Silent. Lifeless. Hopeless.

A senior cop is peeing in the corner as two motorcycles approach.

SENIOR COP
Catch him! Catch him! Stop!

The young cop takes out his earphones. The ambience sound is audible now. He runs to stop the two motorcycles but manages only one; the other escapes. He is frustrated.

YOUNG COP
Don't you know you're not allowed to leave your house? Where is your mask?

BIKER
Sir, I have some very urgent work.

YOUNG COP
Who doesn't have urgent work? And wear your mask!

BIKER
Sir, please let me go.

YOUNG COP
Didn't you hear me? You cannot leave your house. Wear your mask!

SENIOR COP
(still peeing)
Lock him up!

The young cop moves closer to the biker.

BIKER
Don't come closer. Don't—

The young cop moves even closer and grabs his collar.

YOUNG COP
Switch your engine off and get down.

The biker blows a lungful on the young cop's face and kicks him. As the young cop falls, the biker escapes. The senior cop helps the young cop up and pulls him on the side. The dog looks on.

YOUNG COP
Sir, he blew on my face! He had corona for sure!

Becoming suddenly alert, the senior cop leaves him and maintains a distance.

YOUNG COP
Sir, now I'll get corona. I'm going to die.

SENIOR COP
You won't die alone; we are all going to die.

The young cop is shaken by what just happened with him. He sees a scooter approaching.

SENIOR COP
Stop! Stop!

RAJNIKANT
Emergency duty.

SENIOR COP
The whole world is in an emergency. Turn around.

RAJNIKANT
I'm on government duty.

Rajnikant takes out his ID card and shows it to him.

SENIOR COP
What do you do?

RAJNIKANT
I'm a scientist.

SENIOR COP
What do you mean? Like a rocket scientist?

RAJNIKANT
No, I'm a virologist.

SENIOR COP
What?

RAJNIKANT
I'm a virologist.

The senior cop is confused.

SENIOR COP
What kind of science is this?

RAJNIKANT
The science of the virus – like coronavirus. We are the ones finding its cure.

SENIOR COP
Oh, so you are going to save us?

The senior cop laughs sarcastically and turns to the young cop.

SENIOR COP
Come on, get your cure. This guy is going to save us.

(Turning to Rajnikant) He just got corona.

The young cop is getting psyched. He rushes towards Rajnikant.

YOUNG COP
He's making a fool out of you!

The young cop snatches his ID card and throws it away.

YOUNG COP
Get down! Get down! Now squat like a chicken. I said squat like a chicken!

The young cop is furious. He drags him off his scooter.

YOUNG COP
Like a chicken!

RAJNIKANT
Ok, ok, I'll squat like a chicken, man. But why are you getting so mad?

Rajnikant sits in a chicken pose.

YOUNG COP
Now squat!

RAJNIKANT
I'm a scientist. I'm advising you, if you get so angry, corona will catch you quicker.

The young cop breaks down.

YOUNG COP

Do you think we enjoy beating our own people? But you guys don't bloody listen! You can't leave your house means you can't leave your house! Don't you get it?

SENIOR COP

We are all going to die. Watch, we're all going to die.

The senior cop laughs madly. The young cop is psyched; he throws the ID card; the dog looks at it: Indian Council of Medical Research. Just then, sirens fill the emptiness.

2 **EXT. DELHI STREET – NIGHT** 2
**31 December 2019**

The scene closes on a pizza boy riding through the bedecked Delhi city. Hip-hop music leaks through his earphones. People are celebrating the impending turn of the year.

3 **EXT. BALRAM BHARGAVA'S HOUSE – NIGHT** 3

The pizza boy climbs the stairs to reach the second-floor apartment. Parvati, a seventeen-year-old girl, opens the door.

PIZZA BOY

Is this Balram Bhargava's house?

PARVATI

Can you not read the nameplate?

He looks at the nameplate: Dr Balram Bhargava, Director General, Indian Council of Medical Research.

4 **INT. BHARGAVA'S HOUSE – KITCHEN – NIGHT** 4

Parvati carries the pizza to the kitchen. Balram Bhargava, a soft-spoken, cultured man in his late fifties, was making kheer with the help of his cook, Mukundi, Parvati's father.

BALRAM BHARGAVA

Parvati, taste the kheer.

PARVATI

Hmmm, excellent!

BALRAM BHARGAVA

Should I cool it down a bit?

PARVATI

If we cool it down too much, Ammi ji outside is going to heat up.

BALRAM BHARGAVA

That heat is not advisable.

He offers some kheer to gods as prasad.

BALRAM BHARGAVA

नमो ब्रह्माण्ड दवाये (namo brahmand davaye) – say it.

Following the cue, Parvati starts chanting the mantra as Mukundi looks on.

PARVATI

नमो ब्रह्माण्ड दवाये, गो ब्राह्मण हिताय च।
जगत धिताय कृष्णाय, गोविन्दाय नमो नमः॥

namo brahmand-davaaye,
go-braahmand-hitaaya cha
jagad-dhitaaya krishnaaya,
govindaaya namo namah

5 **INT. BALRAM BHARGAVA'S HOUSE – LIVING ROOM – NIGHT** 5

Sunita, Balram's wife, and her two daughters-in-law arrange the table as Balram and Parvati bring the dishes.

Balram's three sons – Raghav, 31, Madhav, 32, and the eldest, Shyam, with his wife – are watching TV.

BALRAM BHARGAVA
Here you go – Lucknow's famous kheer.

PARVATI
And America's 'warm-warm' pizza.

BALRAM BHARGAVA
Look, I made what my mom would feed me in New Year – kheer.

And what your mom would make, you ordered – pizza.

SUNITA BHARGAVA
All good things in the world were only done by your mom.

SHYAM BHARGAVA
I love you-two's style of romance.

Sunita blushes.

Meanwhile, TV shows Chinese people collapsing while in a queue.

BALRAM BHARGAVA
What are we watching?

MADHAV BHARGAVA
Nothing, just fake news.

RAGHAV BHARGAVA
How is it possible that so many people just fall down while standing together!

SHYAM BHARGAVA
They were saying in a video that some virus has leaked from a lab.

PARVATI
In Wuhan.

SUNITA BHARGAVA
The Chinese eat bats...

BALRAM BHARGAVA
So let us have some kheer.

Parvati serves kheer.

SHYAM BHARGAVA
What's happening to Parvati's America plan?

BALRAM BHARGAVA
Well, she has got a scholarship at MIT. She'll join the undergrad programme in September.

SHYAM'S WIFE
Why America? Is there a shortage of good universities in India?

BALRAM BHARGAVA
Well, first of all, she is going to study synthetic virology, and that course is not available in India. Synthetic virology is the future of bioscience, and I hope India can take leadership in this field worldwide. And secondly, I believe you should take in all the knowledge from around

the world and apply it in
your country. And the third
thing ... umm ... What was
the third thing?

SUNITA BHARGAVA
The third thing is that like
every year, this year too,
Mukundi shall play the flute
to bring in the new year.
Parvati, go call your father.

Parvati leaves.

SHYAM'S WIFE
Gotta admit it, a cook's
daughter is going to shape
India's future. Wow!

SUNITA BHARGAVA
After her mother's death, who
does she even have other than
us. She's like our daughter.

BALRAM BHARGAVA
Like? She *is* our daughter.

Mukundi comes with a flute.

DAUGHTER-IN-LAW
Now begins the annual new year
concert, and here is the star
of the show, Mr Mukundi. Let's
kick off the final show of 2019.

Mukundi starts playing '*Raina Beeti Jaaye*'.

PARVATI
Papa, please, not this boring
tune.

SHYAM BHARGAVA
What's wrong? It's R.D.
Burman's best composition.

PARVATI
No, Uncle, please. Today's New year's Eve.

Mukundi passes the flute to her.

MUKUNDI
Well, now, I only know these tunes. Why don't you play something?

PARVATI
Play what?

BALRAM BHARGAVA (sings)
*'Mohabbat karne waale kam na honge/Teri mehfil mein lekin hum na honge'*

Sunita blushes again.

BALRAM BHARGAVA
What's after this? Tell me?

EVERYBODY
After this is 10, 9, 8...

It's a happy moment for the family. Sounds of laughter and fireworks fill the air. Parvati goes to the window and looks outside. The firework display in Delhi's sky is stunning. Welcome 2020.

**6 EXT. DELHI STREET – MORNING 6**
**1 January 2020**

Bhargava is driving down Delhi's empty streets and looking out at what seems like the end of the world. (The camera pans and follows his POV.)

**7 INT. ICMR – DAY 7**

Enna, a young scientist, is pinning New Year cards on her bulletin board when she hears an approaching car. She slides on her chair over to the window to check who it is. She peers out to see Bhargava parking his car.

Bhargava is in a hurry, brisking up his pace as he reads the day's newspaper. A peon keeps up with him and asks him if he could relief him of his stuff, but he refuses. Bhargava can be mistaken for an ordinary person.

He takes the stairs instead of the elevator. On the way to his office room, people wish him Happy New Year. He simply nods as if New Year means nothing.

8 **INT. DIRECTOR GENERAL'S OFFICE – DAY** 8

As Bhargava walks up the corridor, Enna follows him close by.

ENNA

Happy New Year, Sir.

Bhargava reciprocates with a smile, still lost his thought.

ENNA

Sir, the health ministry called. They want to speak to you urgently.

BALRAM BHARGAVA

Connect me.

Bhargava starts making a to-do list as the phone connects with the ministry.

BALRAM BHARGAVA

Bhargava here ... hmmm ... ok ... I'll surely do it.

After he puts on the computer, Bhargava looks up to see Enna watching him.

BALRAM BHARGAVA

Send Nivedita.

ENNA
She's on leave today, Sir.

BALRAM BHARGAVA
Doesn't matter – call her.

Enna starts walking out.

BALRAM BHARGAVA
Enna, happy birthday ...
Happy New Year.

Enna is amused. Perhaps, she is used to it.

Quickly, Bhargava types 'WebCrawler' on Google, which takes him to a WHO post:

'China has reported to World Health Organization a cluster of pneumonia cases in Wuhan in the Hubei Province. Investigations are on to identify the cause.'

**9 EXT. ICMR – DAY 9**

A Suzuki car enters ICMR premises. The peon is waiting at the threshold of the building.

Nivedita Gupta gets out and walks purposefully into the corridor. The peon ushers her into the lift, which takes her to the floor where the DG's office is.

**10 INT. DIRECTOR GENERAL'S OFFICE – DAY 10**

BALRAM BHARGAVA
Nivedita, what took you so long?

NIVEDITA GUPTA
Sir, I was on leave today; I had informed you...

BALRAM BHARGAVA
Hmmm ... Nivedita, In the past few days, the number of

pneumonia cases in China have suddenly increased a lot. On 30 December, they found two pneumonia cases in Brooklyn, which suddenly became ten. A scientist observed a great similarity between the cases in China and America, so she put an alert on WebCrawler.

China was refuting the claims but last night, they reported it themselves.

NIVEDITA GUPTA
What did they say?

BALRAM BHARGAVA
That this might be pneumonia. Might not be. They're calling it an unknown virus that came from Wuhan's seafood market. And Wuhan's Health Commission issued a notice that this is not human-to-human transmission.

NIVEDITA GUPTA
No surprises here. SARS, H5N1, H7N9, bird flu all came from China. What do you expect if you're going to eat so many wild animals?

BALRAM BHARGAVA
What is strange though is that the authorities shut down the market indefinitely.

He looks at her.

NIVEDITA GUPTA
What do you think?

BALRAM BHARGAVA

A valid question is that why isn't there any information about the first case – case zero? And if the first case was found in Wuhan on 1 December, then that means the patient was infected earlier ... in November. That means this unknown virus was brought to the market before it was taken out. Another important question: if the first case was detected on 1 December, why was this information hidden from the world? And don't forget, China's BSL-4 lab is in Wuhan.

NIVEDITA GUPTA

You mean it's a lab leak?

Bhargava is silent, almost vacant, but interrupts himself.

BALRAM BHARGAVA

Let's leave that to Mr Doval. It won't be right for us to speculate.

Nivedita guesses the seriousness of the matter.

BALRAM BHARGAVA

The health ministry has called a conference for a briefing, where WHO will also be represented. You will represent ICMR.

NIVEDITA GUPTA

Ok, Sir. What time is the meeting?

BALRAM BHARGAVA

Ten.

She looks at her watch – it's already 11.30 a.m.

NIVEDITA GUPTA

Sir, it's already eleven-thirty.

BALRAM BHARGAVA

Hmmm ... Not today ... on the 7th ... 7th of January 2020.

NIVEDITA GUPTA

Sir, I dropped everything. I thought it was something urgent. You could have told me this on the phone.

Bhargava thinks for a moment about that possibility.

BALRAM BHARGAVA

You are right. By the way, Happy New Year.

**11 EXT. NEW DELHI – STREET – DAY 11**
**7 January 2020, 10 a.m., Ministry of Health**

The scene opens with a dramatic bird's eye view of New Delhi, reflecting the mundaneness of everyday life. The streets are extremely dense and crowded.

Out amidst the crowd, Nivedita looks on vacantly as people move about shoulder to shoulder happily, unaware of the impending doom. (It amplifies in slow motion.)

DR HANKS (V.O.)

On 31 December 2019, the World Health Organization's China country office was informed of cases of pneumonia due to unknown aetiology detected in Wuhan.

**12 INT. HEALTH MINISTRY – DAY 12**

The scene opens in a high-powered meeting where the WHO representative Dr Hanks is present. (This unfolds from Nivedita's perspective.)

DR HANKS
On 3 January, forty-four cases were reported to the WHO by the Chinese national authorities.

The statistics is alarming and a matter of concern for the World Health Organization.

DR PAUL
Is it human to human transmission?

DR HANKS
Prima facie it seems the virus is zoonotic.

MAN 2
You mean the virus has come from animals?

DR HANKS
Yes, it may have come from Wuhan's seafood market.

MAN 2
The wet market, right?

DR PAUL
I am not convinced about the animal to human transmission.

MAN 3
It has come to my knowledge that the Chinese people eat bats.

MAN 2

Not bats – wild game birds.

MAN 1

Ya, because they have a lot of protein.

MAN 3

SARS also went from bats to civet cats and then came to humans.

DR PAUL

What does your China office say?

DR HANKS

It's very likely that it spread from bats.

NIVEDITA GUPTA

I have been to Wuhan seafood market, and no one sells bats there.

DR HANKS

Maybe it came from a bat to another animal ... from that animal to humans.

NIVEDITA GUPTA

How have you concluded this?

DR HANKS

Our China office informed us.

NIVEDITA GUPTA

Has anyone from WHO's China office inspected the wet market?

DR HANKS

No.

NIVEDITA GUPTA

Have they inspected the P4 lab?

DR HANKS

No, why would they visit the lab?

NIVEDITA GUPTA

Is there a remote possibility of a virus leak from Wuhan's P4 lab?

DR HANKS

No, no, no – no way.

NIVEDITA GUPTA

Then how can you say with so much confidence that its neither human to human nor a lab leak?

DR HANKS

That's what Chinese officials informed our office.

DR PAUL

You mean People's Liberation Army?

A commotion ensues.

DR PAUL

This raises serious security concerns. I think we should make a committee immediately to monitor—

NIVEDITA GUPTA

Monitor what? A case where we haven't been given any information?

Isn't it WHO's responsibility to give us evidence-based scientific research? Unless, of course, they have some special understanding with China.

DR HANKS

What are you hinting at Ms Gupta?

NIVEDITA GUPTA

Dr Gupta.

An awkward moment interrupts.

DR PAUL

Let me ask you Dr Gupta: if this virus spreads out of China and comes to India, will ICMR have what it takes to handle this virus?

NIVEDITA GUPTA

Sir, Indian Council of Medical Research is the oldest vaccine research agency in the world. We're not as popular as ISRO but we're not any lesser than them either.

The committee is humoured.

NIVEDITA GUPTA

Sir, no one can see our achievements because we don't have a rocket whose tail is on fire where everyone is saying, 'Wow, look, it's off to Mars!' If anyone in India has what it takes to fight this virus, it is ICMR.

**13 INT. NIVEDITA GUPTA'S HOUSE – NIGHT 13**

It's dinner time at the Gupta house. Vikas, Nivedita's husband, and their sons – Aditya, 12, and Anant, 10 – are at the dining table, eating, while Nivedita goes in and out of the kitchen, making fresh rotis and supplying them to the dinners.

VIKAS GUPTA

'Rocket whose tail is on fire?' You are too funny.

NIVEDITA GUPTA

Ya, I mean, enough is enough! People can't think beyond rocket scientists. Everyone only wants to send their kids to NASA.

ANANT

I'm going to make rockets like Elon Musk does. Man, rockets are sexy.

NIVEDITA GUPTA

What—

VIKAS GUPTA

He means, rockets are macho.

ADITYA

Dad, that's misogynistic.

NIVEDITA GUPTA

Do you know why majority of the bioscience labs have women? Because people think medical research is a sissy job. What we fight against – a virus – is invisible.

Everyone can see the adventures of a man. 'Look,

that man is going to mars!'
What are we?

ADITYA
Mom, please pass the salt.

NIVEDITA GUPTA
Do what you want, you'll always have to come to your mother to ask for salt. Do you know the iodine that is in this salt was put by us? That alone helped us end goitre and mental retardation. Be it diabetes, cancer, vaccine development, nutrition, occupational health, reproductive health, tribal health, medical statistics, implementation research – Who does all these?

EVERYONE
Of course Mom.

NIVEDITA GUPTA
Well, not just me. All of ICMR. Everyone wants to know what's on Mars, but no one wants to know what is inside us. And this is the biggest problem with us. This Elon Musk—

ANANT
Mumma, please don't bore us.

Vikas hugs Nivedita romantically as Aditya watches them in awkward silence.

VIKAS GUPTA

Nivi, don't be so touchy about ICMR.

NIVEDITA GUPTA

No, I am touchy. I can't hear one thing about my kids and about ICMR.

VIKAS GUPTA

Come on, now, just tell me honestly. If this virus comes to India, will you save us?

NIVEDITA GUPTA

I don't know, but we will try our best.

An indistinct sound of Chinese news fades in.

**14 INT. CHINESE LAB – NIGHT 14**

**11 January 2020, Shanghai Public Health Clinical Center and School of Public Health P3 Lab, CHINA**

CHINESE ANCHOR

Chinese media has reported the first death due to the novel coronavirus.

A sequence of the virus comes alive on the computer screen. A Chinese girl talks with others in a hush-hush tone. They think for a moment and then nod. She attaches a document in an email, types the mailing address, 'Director General, World Health Organization', waits, hesitates and then presses 'enter'.

**15 EXT. GLOBE – NIGHT 15**

The scene pulls back from China to an email being transmitted across the world. It passes through CDC, USA, and spreads all over the world. (The scene overlaps with numerous TV screens and WHO tweets.)

ANCHORS OF VARIOUS NATIONALITIES (V.O.)
Today, Chinese scientists shared the genetic sequence of the novel coronavirus.

**16 EXT. ICMR – DAY 16**
**12 January 2020, ICMR, DELHI**

A long shot of India pans in on Delhi and finally on Enna's desktop where the email lands. The peon looks at Enna checking her email before rushing off to Nivedita, who is walking in the corridor.

Nivedita looks at the sequence and rushes to the DG's office.

ANCHOR (V.O.)
Genetic sequences of the novel coronavirus 2019 (nCoV) will allow countries to develop specific diagnostic kits and ensure better containment of the virus.

**17 INT. DIRECTOR GENERAL'S OFFICE – DAY 17**

Bhargava is on the computer. Nivedita enters the room with Enna following closely behind.

NIVEDITA GUPTA
Sir, open your inbox please.

The inbox leads to an attachment, which brings alive the sequence of the virus.

NIVEDITA GUPTA
Sir, this genome sequence has come from China. It's surrounded by a protective membrane, a protein capsid.

This is not pneumonia. There is no DNA either, only ribonucleic acid.

BALRAM BHARGAVA

This is an RNA virus just like SARS. Looks like this will spread like fire and mutate.

NIVEDITA GUPTA

Thank God, there is no case in India.

BALRAM BHARGAVA

Not yet; please call NIV. I want to talk to Priya Abraham.

**18 INT. NIV, PUNE – DAY 18**

The scene opens in the old colonial HQs of NIV Pune.

Varsha Potdar, 40, is busy on a microscope when her phone rings.

VARSHA POTDAR

Yes, Nivedita. Ok, I'm on it.

Hanging up, Varsha goes down the stairs. She hurries past a gardener who was working on potted plants. The gardener's son follows her with few flowers in hand.

Varsha stops near an ajar door and peeps inside gingerly.

Priya Abraham, the director or NIV, is on FaceTime with her family in Kerala. On the other side is her son, Ananth, would-be daughter-in-law, Merin, and her husband, Dr Abraham Peedicayil.

PRIYA ABRAHAM
I think May is perfect for the wedding.

ANANTH
Mom, May will be very hot. How about February?

Varsha waits awkwardly. The gardener's son is nearby, watching her peep inside the director's room.

(The camera closes in on the FaceTime screen.)

PRIYA ABRAHAM
Na, na, February is too early. I joined just two months ago.

VARSHA POTDAR (on the phone)
Nivi, Priya ma'am is busy on the phone.

NIVEDITA GUPTA
So? Tell her DG sir wants to talk.

Hesitant and awkward, Varsha enters the room.

PRIYA ABRAHAM
I can try March. You check Vellore Army Club. Their AC is strong.

Priya notices Varsha holding the phone.

VARSHA POTDAR
Ma'am, from Delhi.

PRIYA ABRAHAM
Ok, I have to go. I have taken a three-day leave. I am coming to Vellore on 27. Merin, I have to check your wedding gown. Ok, bye.

Priya shifts her focus to Dr Varsha.

VARSHA POTDAR
(handing over the phone to Priya)

Ma'am, DG sir.

Priya takes the phone.

PRIYA ABRAHAM
I am sorry, Sir, I was fixing my son's wedding date.

BALRAM BHARGAVA
That's nice. Great, congrats. Priya ji, please check your email.

Priya opens the mail and looks at the sequence.

BALRAM BHARGAVA
This is the sequence of the novel coronavirus, and it's not looking very comforting. I think NIV should start making its diagnostic kits instantly.

PRIYA ABRAHAM
Ok, Sir. Give us some time.

BALRAM BHARGAVA
This is not the time for some time. I want it immediately. Immediately means—

NIVEDITA GUPTA
Immediately, Sir.

Bhargava cuts the call, and Priya turns to Varsha.

PRIYA ABRAHAM
Is DG sir always in such a hurry?

The gardener's son brings a bunch of flowers and puts it in a vase. Priya smiles at him briefly and looks away at her computer screen.

PRIYA ABRAHAM

We'll have to inform the BSL-4 lab.

**19 EXT. BSL-4 – DAY 19**

A phone rings outside the BSL-4 lab as the scene travels through the BSL-4 lab before focusing on a lady, who enters a room and stops at a desk. Pragya Yadav, the director of BSL-4, NIV, dressed in lab gear, picks up the phone.

PRIYA ABRAHAM

Pragya, I have sent the first genome sequence of the novel coronavirus, which—

PRAGYA YADAV

Ma'am, I was just about to call you. Did you read what South China Morning Post wrote?

Priya is on the computer with the South China Morning Post website opened before her: 'Shanghai Public Health Clinical Center P3 Lab ordered to shut down for ratification.'

PRAGYA YADAV

The lab that shared this genome sequence with the world has been shut down by the authorities. Not just that, Ma'am, the Chinese Health Commission issued a notification, 'letter number 3', which states that all remaining samples of the virus should

be destroyed immediately, and
no information related to it
should be released anywhere.
I have a strange feeling about
this.

Priya is alerted. She is visibly panicking.

PRIYA ABRAHAM
Varsha, please order primers
and probes for testing
this new strain of virus.
Immediately.

**20 VARIOUS TV SETS 20**
**13 January, Thailand**

On a Thai TV (dubbed in Hindi)

THAI ANCHOR
Today the first case of the
novel coronavirus has been
reported outside China in
Thailand. WHO said it is
probable for human to human
transmission in forty-one
confirmed cases.

**16 January, Japan**

JAPANESE ANCHOR
The Japanese health ministry
informed WHO of a confirmed
case of a novel coronavirus
in Japan who travelled to
Wuhan. This was the second
confirmed case detected
outside of China. WHO stated
that considering global
travel patterns, additional
cases in other countries are
likely.

**21 INT. KOLKATA AIRPORT – DAY 21**
**19 January 2020**

A plane lands.

A Kerala girl arrives at the Kolkata airport from Wuhan. At the airport, a group of passengers are watching the news on TV. She joins the crowd.

ANCHOR ROHIT
Welcome to Dangal. I am your host, Rohit. The government of India has taken a big decision ... All passengers flying in from Wuhan will be thermal-scanned.

**22 EXT. BANGALORE RAILWAY STATION – MORNING 22**

A train stops.

The Kerala girl arrives at the Bangalore railway station and walks through thousands of people, coughing slightly.

**23 INT. ICMR CORRIDOR – DAY 23**
**21 January, ICMR, DELHI**

Bhargava paces up the corridor past the peon.

ANCHOR ROHIT (V.O.)
The information provided by China about this unknown virus so far has given rise to more questions than answers.

Nivedita walks into the control room, where Panda, Rajnikant and Dr Ketkar are listening to the news.

ANCHOR ROHIT
Let me remind you, on January 14 WHO said that human to

human transmission of this virus is possible. But on January 19 they said that human to human transmission is not a possibility. And today they took a U-turn and once again said this is human to human transmission. I will let you figure out why WHO is taking such drastic U-turn after U-turn.

Enna joins Bhargava.

ENNA
Sir, we have informed all hospitals and medical centres to send any suspected cases straight to NIV.

Dr Ketkar comes out and notices Bhargava.

KETKAR
Dr Bhargava.

BALRAM BHARGAVA
Yes, Dr Ketkar.

Dr Ketkar goes back in and Bhargava follows him. Enna is close behind. The peon is standing outside watching in.

NIVEDITA GUPTA
Sir, the Wuhan health officials have concluded that this virus came from the Hunan seafood market. And the first criterion for the diagnosis of this virus is that the patient should have gone to the market. So that means if you have a fever and your genome sequence matches

perfectly but you didn't
visit the market, you cannot
be classified as a patient.

BALRAM BHARGAVA
Nothing wrong with that.

Nivedita looks at Dr Ketkar.

KETKAR
Dr Bhargava, after patient zero, on 10 December, three more cases were detected, but two of them had nothing to do with the market.

After that WHO came out with a list of forty-one cases, out of which fourteen cases were found to have not gone to the market. So how did they get infected? After that the *Science* journal posted a report that the Wuhan seafood market may not be the source of the novel virus spreading globally. The *Lancet* also posted a report saying the first case found on 1 December had nothing to do with the seafood market.

BALRAM BHARGAVA
I had my suspicions from day 1.

KETKAR
On 7 January, the National Institute of Communicable Disease Control published a paper, which was run by *Nature* as well. It said the Wuhan coronavirus is matching

exactly with two older viruses, viruses SL-CoVZC45 and SL-CoVZXC21. Both these viruses were sampled from bats in Zhoushan. Do you want to guess who sampled them?

PANDA

People's Liberation Army's Nanjing Military Research Institute. Why would it be a military research institute?

NIVEDITA GUPTA

Sir, what does this similarity indicate?

KETKAR

Does this mean that this virus was reverse engineered in a lab?

An eerie silence descends in the room.

BALRAM BHARGAVA

It would be wrong for us to reach conclusions without any evidence.

NIVEDITA GUPTA

Well, if we are wrong then why did the DG of Wuhan's P4 lab order everyone working in there to not utter a word related to any information, data, results, conclusions, not to mention, a word, to anyone about anything.

RAJNIKANT

It was 'prohibited with immediate effect'.

KETKAR
What does the Chinese Communist Party want to keep hidden from the world?

NIVEDITA GUPTA
Is this a cover-up of the original source?

BALRAM BHARGAVA
Original source?

KETKAR
Is this virus a natural mutation?

NIVEDITA GUPTA
Or was it reverse engineered in a lab?

BALRAM BHARGAVA
This virus is a natural mutation; it was reverse engineered in a lab. I don't know. What's bothering me is why is China's scientific community still quiet?

24 **INT. THRISSUR HOSPITAL – DAY** 24
**23 January 2020**

A taxi stops and the Kerala girl gets off.

A nurse watches as the girl makes her way into the hospital for a check-up. She has problem breathing. Doctors are alerted immediately.

They collect the sample from her nose and throat and label it for dispatch: To, NIV, PUNE.

**25 INT. BSL-4 LAB – DAY 25**
**27 January 2020**

Sri Laxmi, a scientist, watches a sample being delivered in an NIV van. She takes it to Pragya Yadav, who is in the lab with Anita, Reema and other scientists.

PRAGYA YADAV
Have we completed all the protocols?

SRI LAXMI
Yes, Ma'am.

PRAGYA YADAV
Send some samples to BSL-2 – to Varsha's lab. BSL-2 will be team 1 and BSL-4 will be team 2. Till both the results don't match, we won't conclude anything.

Sri Laxmi starts whispering something with folded hands.

PRAGYA YADAV
What happened?

SRI LAXMI
Just praying, Ma'am. This is the first time in my life that I am wishing for a negative result.

**26 INT. PRIYA'S VELLORE HOUSE – EVENING 26**
**29 January, 7 p.m.**

The scene opens with a beautiful shot of Merin in her wedding gown.

PRIYA ABRAHAM

This is so beautiful –
Gorgeous!

ANANTH

Mom, confirm the date. We Will have to pay the advance by the thirty-first if we want the Vellore club.

PRIYA ABRAHAM

Feb I can't. There will be a lot of heat on me. Anyway people don't like me much at NIV.

MERIN

Why, Aunty?

DR ABRAHAM

Now you can call her mummy.

MERIN

Mummy.

PRIYA ABRAHAM

That's so sweet I'll cry. Lifelong I've been a practicing doctor. This is an administration job. I need a while to adjust.

MERIN

Ok, I am happy with March. Papa?

DR ABRAHAM

I am just a surgeon, not as busy as your mummy. March is fine with me.

Priya's phone rings. Merin picks it. It's Varsha.

PRIYA ABRAHAM
Yes, Varsha?

VARSHA
Ma'am, we think...

A long pause ensued. Priya takes a deep breath.

PRIYA ABRAHAM
We think what?

VARSHA
Ma'am, we think we have a positive.

Priya rests against a wall. Takes another deep breath.

PRIYA ABRAHAM
Ok, nobody should panic. Stay very calm. I'll be right there.

Everyone is looking at her, worried.

MERIN
What happened, Mummy?

PRIYA ABRAHAM
We will have to postpone the wedding.

DR ABRAHAM
Ananth, God is giving you a second chance to think about your wedding.

ANANTH
Till when?

PRIYA ABRAHAM
Can't say. Get the car out. I have to go to the airport.

27 **INT. NIV, PUNE – NIGHT** 27
**30 January 2020, 2 a.m.**

The gardener's son wakes up to the sound of Priya's car entering. He looks at the car being pulled over. Varsha runs to the balcony and sees Priya getting down. The gardener's son switches the light on for Priya, and she rushes up to the lab. Through the window, the gardener's son sees the whole team waiting. They show Priya the 3D results on computer.

PRIYA ABRAHAM
What about team 2's results at BSL-4?

VARSHA
They haven't shared the results.

28 **EXT. PUNE – THE MAGIC HOUR** 28
**5 a.m.**

A jogger sees a few cars passing against backdrop of an indigo sky.

29 **INT. BSL-4 LAB – SUNRISE** 29

Sri Laxmi watches as the cars enter the premises.

Priya and her team are being screened through the strictest protocols.

Priya crosses the corridors and sees through the glass windows that scientists are busy and tense. She puts on lab gear and goes into the room as Sri Laxmi looks through the glass window from outside. Pragya takes Priya to the microscope.

Priya peers through the microscope (intense music picks up in the background).

PRIYA ABRAHAM

It's a beautiful virus. So royal. And the crown on its head is majestic. No wonder it's called corona. Wow! We got you, Your Highness Corona.

Sri Laxmi, Anita, Reema and the team wait in anticipation.

PRIYA ABRAHAM

So, girls, It's matching with the Chinese sequence. It is indeed Severe Acute Respiratory Syndrome Coronavirus-2. Good work, everyone.

Anita writes 'patient 0' on the report. Priya now realises the gravity of the situation. She breathes heavily, sweating.

PRIYA ABRAHAM

Oh my God! Now what?

**30 EXT. BSL-4 – MORNING 30**

Priya walks out surrounded by her colleagues. Her phone rings from an unknown number. She hands it over to Varsha.

PRIYA ABRAHAM

How will we inform DG sir?

PRAGYA YADAV

Don't be nervous, Ma'am. We will handle it?

PRIYA ABRAHAM

Let's meet at NIV at nine.

Her phone rings again from an unknown number. She again hands it over to Varsha.

PRIYA ABRAHAM
Please check, Varsha. Pragya, find out how many reagents you have, how many samples we can test, how many labs we can send the reagents to, how many PPE kits do we have. Let's check the results again.

PRAGYA YADAV
Ma'am, It's 100 per cent correct. Our team has worked day and night for a zero-error result. It's a great achievement by our team.

PRIYA ABRAHAM
I know, I know, Pragya. The irony is that our scientific achievements are bad news for the world. We virologists are bad-news messengers for the world.

VARSHA POTDAR
Ma'am, journalist—

PRIYA ABRAHAM
Who?

VARSHA POTDAR
Some Rohini Singh Dhulia, science editor from the Daily Wire.

PRIYA ABRAHAM
I am busy. I can't talk to the media right now.

VARSHA POTDAR
Ma'am is busy.

Varsha cuts the phone. The phone rings again. She cuts the phone again. The phone rings again. Relentless. Priya loses it.

PRIYA ABRAHAM

She told you na? I am busy. And it's six in the morning. Is this the time to call someone?

ROHINI SINGH DHULIA

You have also reached the BSL-4 lab at five in the morning. We're all working in the national interest. Can I ask you few questions?

PRIYA ABRAHAM

I am not obliged to talk to the media. Please don't waste my time and don't call again. You understand? Wait, where did you say you are from? Wire? What Wire? Daily Wire? I have never heard this name?

ROHINI SINGH DHULIA

It has been rumoured that the first case of India has been found in Kerala.

Priya panics and looks at Pragya on the other side of the phone.

ROHINI SINGH DHULIA

Why Kerala? Why not UP? So that the central government can blame Kerala for this outbreak?

PRIYA ABRAHAM

What kind of question is this? Are you seriously a science editor?

PRAGYA YADAV
Ma'am, avoid.

PRIYA ABRAHAM
No, she must know. Because Kerala has the best medical infrastructure; they have had outbreaks like Nipah, so they have medical intelligence.

ROHINI SINGH DHULIA
Will India evacuate its citizens from China? Does India have the capability to quarantine so many people?

PRIYA ABRAHAM
I don't have any answers to your stupid questions. Bye.

Priya cuts the phone.

PRIYA ABRAHAM
Who is this Rohini Singh ... what ... Pulla ... Pulia?

VARSHA POTDAR
Dhulia.

PRIYA ABRAHAM
Whatever. Who makes them a science editor? Stupid people.

PRAGYA YADAV
She is not stupid. She knows where the first case was found, what time, who to call. She's following us very closely. Only two people follow someone so closely – friends or enemies.

The Daily Wire headline flashes on the TV: 'Government has no answers,' says the NIV director on the corona preparedness.

31 **INT. BALRAM BHARGAVA'S HOUSE – DAY** 31

The dining table is set. TV plays in the background.

ANCHOR ROHIT

WHO's director general Tedros Adhanom Ghebreyesus has declared corona as a public health emergency of international concern today.

India's prime minister has directed that all arrangements be made under the Vande Bharat mission to bring back Indians residing abroad immediately.

SUNITA BHARGAVA

Where is this man? Paru, go call him.

Parvati walks past Bhargava's room. She sees Bhargava staring at the Daily Wire report on his laptop. Eventually, he makes a call.

BALRAM BHARGAVA

Sir, we have got our first case.

Silence.

CABINET SECRETARY

Oh God! Let me inform the PMO.

Silence.

CABINET SECRETARY

Dr Bhargava, what has your director of NIV told the

media? That the government
has no answers?

BALRAM BHARGAVA

Sir, Dr Abraham didn't say
that. All she said was—

CABINET SECRETARY

What difference does it make
what she said when you know
very well that the media
writes the headline first and
then fits the half-truth into
it. They have no concern
about corona.

They only want India's
COVID-19 management to fail
somehow so that their agenda
can succeed. Please tell Dr
Abraham to stay away from
sensationalising during such
a critical time.

BALRAM BHARGAVA

Yes.

CABINET SECRETARY

In the meantime, make a
WhatsApp group. The PM wants
to know the progress minute
by minute.

BALRAM BHARGAVA

Sir, I don't have WhatsApp.

CABINET SECRETARY

The whole world is in such a
crisis, and you don't have
WhatsApp? You serious?

Parvati runs and sits on her chair.

ANCHOR ROHIT

The Pakistani government has instructed its students residing in China to stay in Wuhan because Pakistan cannot treat coronavirus.

Bhargava shuts the TV. He behaves as if everything is normal.

BALRAM BHARGAVA

Focus on your food. Tell me, which mobile is the best for WhatsApp? And put ghee in your kadhi. You want to be a scientist? Your mind needs to be strong. Ghee is good for that.

PARVATI

iPhone.

SUNITA BHARGAVA

Everything ok?

BALRAM BHARGAVA

Ya ... no, tell me something cheaper.

SUNITA BHARGAVA

You've become the director general but you're still afraid of spending.

BALRAM BHARGAVA

To have less needs and to not waste doesn't mean I am afraid to spend.

(To Parvati)

Why are you eating with a spoon? Kadhi chawal should always be eaten with your hands. It tastes better that way. Humans have increased their needs to such extents that even the earth is seeming small.

Naturally, now nature will reduce these needs, and then everyone will cry. Also, eat Kaddu; it has medicinal properties. The older generations were right: live a simple life and have big thoughts. By the way, what is the difference between iOS and Android.

Sunita observes silently that Bhargava's mind is elsewhere.

**32 INT. THE DAILY WIRE OFFICE – DAY 32**

A woman walks into the office with a powerful gait. She is Rohini Singh Dhulia, poised, courageous and fierce, sipping her Starbucks coffee as she makes heads turn.

Four assistants follow her with files, documents, tablets, etc., trying to catch up with her.

ASSISTANT 1

Ma'am, India is ranked 57th in the health index, even behind Indonesia.

ROHINI SINGH DHULIA

You mean at the bottom? What about other data?

ASSISTANT 2

According to Government of India's data, we have only eight doctors for every 10,000 people.

ROHINI SINGH DHULIA
And ICU beds?

ASSISTANT 3
Only six ICU beds for one lakh people.

ROHINI SINGH DHULIA
Yes, let's build more temples! What about PPE kits?

ASSISTANT 1
Ma'am, India doesn't make PPE kits at all, and according to Government of India, we have only 2.75 lakh imported PPE kits.

ROHINI SINGH DHULIA
This is how we will become a world guru? What about masks?

ASSISTANT 2
We don't make masks either, and as of now, we have just 3.35 lakh N-95 masks.

ROHINI SINGH DHULIA
Wow! We stand with everyone, and we stand for everyone! What about ventilators?

ASSISTANT 4
There is acute short supply of ventilators too. All of India has just 48,000 ventilators.

ROHINI SINGH DHULIA
Wow, a country set to become a five-trillion-dollar economy is not on course to become the largest funeral ground on

earth. We are a dead country.
India can't do it!

33 **INT. THE DAILY WIRE OFFICE, NEWSROOM – DAY** 33

Rohini is in her chair while her make up is being done. Soon, her casual look is transformed into one of professional. Her assistant brings her a sandwich.

ROHINI SINGH DHULIA
Is it vegan?

ASSISTANT 2
Yes, Ma'am.

The editor approaches Rohini.

EDITOR
Are you out of your mind, Rohini? How can you say this?

Why don't you talk about China and the origin of this virus?

ROHINI SINGH DHULIA
(Calm and assertive) Because, you know, we can't.

EDITOR
So now you'll say India can't do it? How can we say this?

ROHINI SINGH DHULIA
Because it is the truth.

EDITOR
No, it's your opinion.

ROHINI SINGH DHULIA
Ok, we can say 'experts' believe India can't do it.

EDITOR
But we haven't spoken to any experts.

ROHINI SINGH DHULIA
Doesn't matter. If we do, this is what they will say: India can't do it. Trust me.

EDITOR
You're a science editor, not a political editor!

ROHINI SINGH DHULIA
Everything is politics, Boss. Even science.

EDITOR
What if you are wrong?

Rohini smiles seductively. She picks up her sandwich and looks at her assistant.

ROHINI SINGH DHULIA
You sure this sandwich is vegan?

ASSISTANT 1
Yes, Ma'am.

TECHNICIAN
Going live in 5, 4, 3, 2—.

ROHINI SINGH DHULIA
Hello friends, I'm Rohini Singh Dhulia, and welcome to my show. In China, 132 people have lost their lives due to the coronavirus. In America, two cases have been reported. France and Italy have reported three cases each. And in the UK, one death has

been registered. Currently, there is only one case in India, but can we be certain there is just one case? How can we, considering we don't even have labs to test this virus.

When I spoke to the experts and asked them if India can fight this epidemic, their answer was a clear and confident no. Deep in your hearts, I know, you're thinking the same thing. Is India's medical infrastructure capable of saving the lives of 1.3 billion people? If we go by what the experts say, the only answer before us is no: India can't do it!

**34 INT. ICMR CONTROL ROOM – DAY 34**

The ICMR team is watching Rohini reporting the news.

KETKAR

How do we handle this?

BALRAM BHARGAVA

Like a war.

All heads turn to face the DG.

**35 INT. TV SET – DAY 35**
**11 February 2020**

The news is playing in several international languages:

VARIOUS ANCHORS

WHO announced that the International Committee on Taxonomy of Virus has named the virus as SARS-COV2, and the disease caused by the novel coronavirus would be named COVID-19.

**14 February 2020**

ANCHOR ROHIT

Today, the first death from COVID-19 occurred in France. This is the fourth death outside China and the first COVID-related death outside Asia. So far, COVID-19 has claimed the lives of 1,500 people in China.

**23 February 2020**

VARIOUS ANCHORS

Europe faced its first major outbreak as the number of reported cases in Italy grew from fewer than five to more than 150. In Italy, officials locked down ten towns.

Schools have been closed and all sports and cultural events are cancelled.

36 **INT. BALRAM BHARGAVA'S HOUSE – NIGHT** 36

**27 February 2020, 12 a.m.**

Bhargava wears his shoes. He peeps in to see Sunita sleeping. As he sneaks out gingerly, Parvati watches him leave.

BALRAM BHARGAVA
If amma ji asks, tell her I have gone for a walk.

SUNITA BHARGAVA (O.S.)
Ask babu ji to take the keys. He doesn't have to wake up the whole house when he comes back.

PARVATI
You're wearing leather shoes to walk?

Bhargava asks her to keep quiet.

37 **EXT. DELHI STREETS – NIGHT** 37

KETKAR
Why has the cabinet secretary called us for a meeting at twelve?

BALRAM BHARGAVA
I don't know. He said, let's meet and talk. Might want to know about our preparedness.

KETKAR
Or our opinion.

BALRAM BHARGAVA
What opinion?

KETKAR
About the origin of this virus.

NIVEDITA GUPTA
It's not the seafood market; I'll tell you that. They

tested each and every animal in the market and didn't find a shred of evidence.

BALRAM BHARGAVA
But there is no evidence that it was leaked from the lab. And how does it matter where it came from? A pandemic is imminent.

NIVEDITA GUPTA
It matters because the origin will tell us how to tackle it.

KETKAR
This virus is not natural.

Everyone pays attention.

KETKAR
This is a fact that the coronavirus is in bats. So how did it come to humans?

BALRAM BHARGAVA
They're cutting trees ... the bats are coming to the cities. It's all there.

KETKAR
No Sir, the virus that infects a bat cannot infect humans. To infect humans, it would need many intermediary species. It takes hundreds or maybe thousands of years for an animal virus to learn how to infect humans.

The bat-originated coronavirus was discovered

in Chinese mines only eight years ago. So, was this thousand-year process artificially shortened in a laboratory?

BALRAM BHARGAVA
You mean 'gain of function'?

NIVEDITA GUPTA
Yes, Sir. Gain-of-function research has been going on at the P4 lab in Wuhan for the past several years with funding from America and France. This means that the viruses that do not naturally exist were being synthetically created.

Silence.

NIVEDITA GUPTA
I am convinced as well. This isn't natural.

A car stops at South Block.

NIVEDITA GUPTA
Sir, if a virus spreads too fast, it can't be fatal like the flu or a cold. And if it is fatal, it can't spread easily like HIV. But COVID-19 is spreading fast and it is killing. It's going against the very laws of virology.

KETKAR
Sir, we should tell the cabinet secretary collectively so he can inform the PM.

BALRAM BHARGAVA
I think it's better if we leave that to Ajit Doval. We should do the things only we can do.

**38 INT. CABINET SECRETARY'S OFFICE – NIGHT 38**

A slide shows satellite images of mass graves in Iran.

CABINET SECRETARY
After China, COVID has spread the most in Iran, and the highest number of deaths have also occurred there. If the satellite photos of mass graves are true, it poses a big challenge for us. Dr Bhargava, 1,100 people from Kargil who went for hajj are stuck in a place called Qom, near Tehran.

KETKAR
Qom? What's Qom. Don't they go to Mecca?

CABINET SECREATARY
Those are Sunnis. Shia people go to Qom. Apart from them, there are 6,000 Indians living in Iran. The PMO has given strict orders to safely evacuate all Indians through the Vande Bharat mission, but the problem is that there are no testing labs in Iran.

NIVEDITA GUPTA
Bringing them back without testing would only put the country at risk.

CABINET SECRETARY

If ICMR can establish a lab there, then we can bring them back.

BALRAM BHARGAVA

Establishing a lab is not a joke. We'll need machinery, transportation, scientists...

CABINET SECRETARY

Let me know what we can do.

BALRAM BHARGAVA

Sir, we don't have time, and we don't have the experience.

The map of Iran flashes on the screen.

CABINET SECRETARY

Dr Bhargava, these are the five cities where our citizens are stuck. You will have to make five teams and establish a lab. Iran is a very complex and sensitive country.

ICMR has to bring back 6,000 Indian people from Iran by testing them with great caution and great care. And you don't have an option.

Bhargava looks at Nivedita. Ketkar is not happy with the decision. On a piece of paper he had written 'GOF research Wuhan lab'. He crumples it up and slides it into his pocket.

**39 INT. BSL-4 LAB – DAY 39**

Priya, Varsha, Pragya, Anita, Reema (pregnant), Gajanand, Sri Laxmi, Manohar are present.

MANOHAR
Iran? No, Ma'am, I won't go to Iran.

Pragya is watching carefully. (The scene unfolds from her POV.)

PRIYA ABRAHAM
Why?

MANOHAR
No, Ma'am, not Iran. I'll go anywhere else but not Iran.

REEMA
Ma'am, I'll go to Iran.

Priya looks at her pregnant belly.

VARSHA POTDAR
Ma'am, I can go.

All the women present agree to go. Priya looks at them with surprise and then looks at Pragya.

**40 INT. PRAGYA'S HOUSE – NIGHT 40**

An old couple waits for Sanjay, Pragya's husband, who walks up the stairs in his army uniform, carrying bananas. He gives the bananas to the old couple.

OLD COUPLE
Thank you, Doctor. Live happily, Arjun.

SANJAY
Uncle, Arjun is your son; I'm Dr Sanjay, your neighbour.

OLD WIFE
Where is Arjun?

Sanjay has no answer.

Sanjay enters his apartment. His daughter is studying.

SANJAY
Put your eye drop.

The daughter nods. He sees Pragya packing.

SANJAY
What's all this?

PRAGYA YADAV
I have to go to Iran with a team.

SANJAY
Iran? Are you out of your mind?

PRAGYA YADAV
Why? When you went to Kargil, did I say you were out of your mind?

There is silence. Pragya goes to the kitchen and brings a dish.

PRAGYA YADAV
I have made maathe waale aalo. Tell me is it bitter?

SANJAY YADAV
Do you have to go at such a time?

They look at each other. Pragya is determined.

PRAGYA YADAV
I'm going, Sanjay.

**41 INT. NIV, PUNE – DAY 41**
**28 February 2020**

A video conferenced is on.

PRIYA ABRAHAM
Sir, I don't think we should send women. It's Iran.

BALRAM BHARGAVA
I don't differentiate between men and women. We're all scientists.

NIVEDITA GUPTA
Sir, you don't differentiate but they do. No matter how idealistic we are, we cannot ignore some social realities.

BALRAM BHARGAVA
It's the PMO we are talking about, Priya ji. If they are saying you have to go, you have to go.

PRIYA ABRAHAM
Sir, the PM is a single man. He doesn't know what women go through. We're scientists not soldiers. Even the army doesn't send it's women to high-risk zones.

BALRAM BHARGAVA
So send the men.

PRIYA ABRAHAM
Sir, there are only women at NIV. How many males do we even have. And the ones we have, they're kids, Sir. As a team leader, I feel responsible for them. If anything happens to them then...

Bhargava is irritated.

BALRAM BHARGAVA
Look, Dr Priya, you have three options. First, send a team. Second, write a letter to the cabinet secretary that you cannot send a team. And third, I'm sorry you do not have a third option.

**42 INT. NIVEDITA GUPTA'S HOUSE – NIGHT 42**

Nivedita Gupta's son Aditya is telling her about Thor, but she is busy in her own work. Her laptop is on: 'After Latin America, the United States reported first corona death.'

Anant is observing it.

ADITYA
Mumma, I've been telling you about Thor for so long. Hello, are you even listening?

NIVEDITA GUPTA
Of course, of course.

ADITYA
Ok, so tell me what I just said?

Nivedita Gupta is blank.

VIKAS GUPTA
Why are you so busy? Are you the prime minister?

Nivedita realises she can't escape. She shuts the laptop.

NIVEDITA GUPTA
Sorry, sorry, sorry. Mumma is so sorry. Now tell me. You have all my attention.

Aditya starts to talk. Her phone rings. It's Bhargava.

NIVEDITA GUPTA
Yes, Sir.

BALRAM BHARGAVA
Tell the NIV team that I want everyone in my office tomorrow morning.

43 **INT. DIRECTOR GENERAL'S OFFICE – DAY** 43

The entire team is waiting for Bhargava.

PRIYA ABRAHAM
Man, why are ACs off?

PANDA
DG sir doesn't like ACs.

KETKAR
He wants you to feel the heat.

PRIYA ABRAHAM
Well, why don't we call for heaters then.

Bhargava enters.

BALRAM BHARGAVA
Dr Priya, the cabinet secretary called me. Did you really send him a letter?

PRIYA ABRAHAM
But, Sir, you only told me to send a letter.

BALRAM BHARGAVA
To hell with your letter! He said you're fired! Fired!

They have never seen him so furious.

BALRAM BHARGAVA

You think this is a wedding, Dr Priya? If your house is on fire, do you debate who should get the water – a man or a woman? This is war!

And we all are soldiers. And what is the first duty of a soldier? To protect the people of their nation. What will happen if we go to Iran? We might die, but should we let 6,000 Indians die abroad just to save ourselves? Is this a soldier?

Pin drop silence.

BALRAM BHARGAVA

A soldier's duty is to take commands. Whose commands? Their general's. And who is your general? Look at me, everyone! If anyone has any doubts, they can leave right now. From this day onwards, everyone should focus only on the fish eye just like Arjun. Understood? Only the fish eye. And in this war, the eye of the fish is saving the life of every Indian.

He takes a deep breath.

BALRAM BHARGAVA

And this is only possible when you have conviction and commitment. Be it a man or a woman.

He writes on a whiteboard: conviction and commitment.

BALRAM BHARGAVA
Is that clear?

44 **INT. DELHI STREET – DAY** 44

Priya and Pragya travel in a cab in silence. Priya is breathing heavily. Suddenly, Priya starts crying. Pragya consoles her.

PRAGYA YADAV
Ma'am, I'll ready a team. You take it easy.

Priya nods.

PRIYA ABRAHAM
By the way, what is this *machli ki aankh* story? I did not understand.

The cab stops at the airport.

45 **INT. ICMR CONTROL ROOM – DAY** 45

On a video conference:

Six young and nervous men sit next to Priya.

PRIYA ABRAHAM
Sir, the team for Iran is ready, but there is a problem. They don't have passports.

KETKAR
How is it possible? Who doesn't have a passport?

Bhargava calls the cabinet secretary.

BALRAM BHARGAVA
Sir, we need some very urgent passports and custom clearance for our equipment.

(To Ketkar)

Only 6 per cent of our population has a passport ... only 6.

(Back to call)

Yes, Sir, the flight's tomorrow morning at eleven. They will be ready.

BALRAM BHARGAVA
It's all done. Priya ji, please pack all your equipment by tomorrow morning. Flight is at 11 a.m.

PRIYA ABRAHAM
Tomorrow morning?

BALRAM BHARGAVA
Fifty people work at your NIV. If a team of five works throughout the night, they won't die. They should be packed and ready by tomorrow morning.

**46 EXT. NIV, PUNE – NIGHT 46**

The gardener's son helps the team of technicians pack the equipment. He sees Priya walking home, talking on FaceTime.

PRIYA ABRAHAM
We will have to postpone the wedding. Iran has made

me crazy. I am trying to coordinate flight bookings, passports, visas, packing...

DR ABRAHAM

You're doing all this?

PRIYA ABRAHAM

Who else will?

DR ABRAHAM

Priya, are you the director of NIV or the operations manager?

PRIYA ABRAHAM

Honestly, a slave!

Priya notices a female scientist is breastfeeding her baby while packing.

PRIYA ABRAHAM

You know it's illegal to get kids in NIV? It's a biosecure zone.

FEMALE SCIENTIST

Ma'am, I know, but we have to pack. I couldn't drop her home.

I am a single mother. I have to breastfeed, so I got her.

PRIYA ABRAHAM

How old is she?

FEMALE SCIENTIST

Six months.

PRIYA ABRAHAM

It's late. You should go home.

FEMALE SCIENTIST

Ma'am, if we don't pack the stuff, we won't go tomorrow.

PRIYA ABRAHAM

What's her name?

FEMALE SCIENTIST

Aasha.

PRIYA ABRAHAM

Nice name. When she grows up, tell her the story of Arjun's *machli ki aankh*. Give Aasha to me. I'll take her home and put her to sleep. When it's time to feed her, come home.

Priya carries the baby to her house.

**47 EXT. NIV WAREHOUSE – DAY 47**
**2 March 2020**

Priya hands over passports to the departing colleagues. They are standing in front of a van as equipment is being loaded. Pragya and Varsha are present to see them off.

PRIYA ABRAHAM

All the best.

Priya notices a technician with a pair of slippers.

PRIYA ABRAHAM

You'll go like this in slippers?

TECHNICIAN

Ma'am, I don't have shoes.

She can't believe it. She takes out some money and gives it to him.

PRIYA ABRAHAM

Go now and buy a pair.

All of them touch her feet. Gururaj does the same.

PRIYA ABRAHAM
Hey, come on now – no, no, no. Alright, fine, touch. God bless you. Now run.

**48 INT. NIV, PUNE – NIGHT 48**

Varsha rushes to Priya's office, but the latter isn't there. She sees her going downstairs.

VARSHA POTDAR
Ma'am, they missed their flight.

PRIYA ABRAHAM
What? How?

VARSHA POTDAR
The equipment was overweight; they didn't have the money to pay for excess luggage.

PRIYA ABRAHAM
They should've used their credit cards and got it reimbursed.

VARSHA POTDAR
Ma'am, they don't have credit cards.

Priya stands still like a statue. She calls the DG.

BALRAM BHARGAVA
I heard what happened. Why didn't anyone go to drop them?

PRIYA ABRAHAM
Sir, everyone was busy packing.

BALRAM BHARGAVA

I'm shocked your scientists don't even have one lakh rupees.

PRIYA ABRAHAM

Not my scientists, Sir, India's scientists.

She looks down; the gardener's son is standing with a flower.

**49 EXT. TEHRAN AIRPORT – MORNING 49**

**3 March 2020**

(Few shots of Tehran.)

**50 INT. TEHRAN CITY HOSPITAL – DAY 50**

In a hall in a Tehran hospital, an Indian flag flutters behind a makeshift lab. A placard reads 'ICMR + NIV Vande Bharat COVID-19 Iran Mission'. The hall is full of desperate people.

Slowly, some locals come in and start shouting and arguing with hospital officials, scaring a young technician.

The hospital manager comes and explains to the Indian envoy, who translates it for Gururaj and his team.

INDIAN ENVOY

These are local residents who are saying that we cannot conduct tests here. They are saying that it could spread COVID in their neighbourhood, and there is no treatment for it.

We will have to stop this operation.

GURURAJ
How can we just stop it?

INDIAN ENVOY
We have no option.

GURURAJ
Sir, give us a place in some small clinic, but don't stop this operation.

The Indian envoy appreciates his commitment and smiles.

**51 INT. TEHRAN, ISOLATED HOSPITAL – DAY 51**

(The scene opens with a long shot of an isolated Iranian village.)

An old Iranian man watches few buses stop. People get down.

GURURAJ
We are ready. Everybody, now one by one. Not like this. Maintain social distancing.

Nobody cares for the protocol. There is panic.

The old Iranian man observes the team taking swab samples, marking them and placing them into a box. One team member notes the names.

Hundreds of people are being tested for COVID-19.

Suddenly, a commotion from outside leaks into the room. The old Iranian man looks outside. Gururaj joins him. Armed Iranian revolutionary guards had stopped the operation.

DIPLOMAT 1
The people are getting mad; we will have to run.

GURURAJ

But our equipment...

DIPLOMAT

You will get your equipment again but not your life.

As the team runs for dear life, one of the technicians freezes over from being too scared. Gururaj realises that the samples had been left behind; he rushes back to get them. On seeing him suddenly appear, the technician screams his lungs out from fear.

TECHNICIAN

They'll kill me! They'll kill me!

GURURAJ

Take all the samples and run!

Gururaj grabs the technician and runs. The militiamen are after them. The technician gets so scared that he pees in his pants as he runs.

The old Iranian man watches the van leave. Inside the van, the young technician breaks down.

**52 INT. VARIOUS PLACES – NIGHT 52**

Everyone is on a video call from their homes and offices.

BALRAM BHARGAVA

I have spoken to the ambassador. The Indian embassy is our territory. We can set up a lab there.

GURURAJ

But, Sir, our equipment has been left behind.

KETKAR

How will they set up a lab without equipment?

PRIYA ABRAHAM

May I suggest something? You don't need a lab. Just have the samples sent to NIV, we will test them overnight. Pragya?

PRAGYA YADAV

Of course, Ma'am, I will generate the SoP immediately.

NIVEDITA GUPTA

*Meri air force se baat ho gayi*. I have spoken with the air force. Positive cases will be brought back in special flights and quarantined in Delhi's air force facility.

PANDA

Even the army has started its Samudra Setu Mission. They'll evacuate a hundred people as well.

BALRAM BHARGAVA

Good. I like the teamwork. If there is any problem, my WhatsApp is working 24/7.

NIVEDITA GUPTA

Sir, WhatsApp?

BALRAM BHARGAVA

Ya, WhatsApp. What's the big deal?

In a rare moment of stolen relief under pressure, all of them smile.

53 **EXT. TEHRAN INDIAN EMBASSY – DAY** 53

A basement has been converted into a hospital facility. The young technician is seen in the middle of a scurry of activities. He looks on as hundreds of tests are being done.

GURURAJ

Sir, samples are ready to be sent.

DIPLOMAT

Samples can only go at night.

GURURAJ

But this is urgent!

The diplomat takes him to the window. The technician follows them. Outside, a huge crowd is protesting.

GURURAJ

Who are they?

AMBASSADOR AKASH WANKHEDE

Pakistanis. They are protesting against CAA.

GURURAJ

I understand them, but the people protesting in Shaheen Bagh in India are not Pakistanis.

The technician is back to work. He goes from one face to the next of very sick people. The entire scene is of chaos and human suffering. He comes face to face with a very old man, whose young daughter holds his hand.

YOUNG GIRL

Please save my dad.

Surge with intense emotion, the technician runs into the bathroom and cries in front of the mirror.

**54 INT. BSL-4 LAB – DAY 54**

Samples begin arriving at NIV. Pragya and the team start testing them. The count is being checked and verified.

**55 INT. NIVEDITA OFFICE – NIGHT 55**

The peon walks past Nivedita's office; she is busy on her computer. She notices a mismatch in the sample count. While the record shows that forty-two samples had been sent, only forty reports were entered.

**56 INT. PRIYA'S HOUSE – NIGHT 56**

A phone rings, disturbing the peace. The gardener's son sees Priya's window lit up.

NIVEDITA GUPTA

Priya ji, we sent you forty-two Iran samples, but we only have the results of forty.

PRIYA ABRAHAM

Oh my God! Let me check.

**57 EXT. NIV, PUNE – NIGHT 57**

The gardener's son watches as Priya rushes to her office. She calls Varsha, who wakes up and picks her phone.

PRIYA ABRAHAM

Varsha, there is a crisis. Come here with Gajanand immediately.

She opens the lock of her office and finds some papers. She hears a car arriving and rushes out.

PRIYA ABRAHAM
How may samples did you test?

VARSHA POTDAR
Forty, Ma'am.

PRIYA ABRAHAM
But the list is of forty-two samples.

VARSHA POTDAR
We only got forty, Ma'am.

PRIYA ABRAHAM
Varsha, these are high profile samples. We can't lose them.

The gardener's son observes as Priya, Varsha and Gajanad search for the missing samples. Priya calls Nivedita.

PRIYA ABRAHAM
If we don't find those samples and COVID spreads, everyone will blame us. They'll question our biosafety. The DG is always ready to shoot me for anything. We will be hanged.

Priya looks at the sky, pacing up and down.

PRIYA ABRAHAM
And everyone believes that we cannot handle testing, and the media is just focused on how to crucify Priya Abraham. Missing samples are like lost bio-bombs. Oh my God, I have screwed it!

Gajanand calls her from behind. He is holding a tube.

GAJANAND

Ma'am, I found both samples.

Priya stands in disbelief.

GAJANAND

It was our mistake. Before sterilization, they put it in the autoclave, right? They got stuck there with the tape.

PRIYA ABRAHAM

How can we make such a stupid mistake? How, how? ... I mean...

She is exhausted. Priya sits on a small rock, numb. The gardener's son offers her a bottle of water.

PRIYA ABRAHAM

What's your name?

GARDENER'S SON

Krishna.

She looks at him with gratitude.

**58 INT. ICMR CONTROL ROOM – NIGHT 58**

On a video call:

Bhargava, Nivedita, Priya, Pragya, Enna and others watch an evacuation report on TV. The visual is of Iran's map, showing 2,028 samples from five cities. According to the report, 308 (15%) samples tested positive for SARS-CoV-2.

PRAGYA YADAV

Who would've thought that we will be able to test and safely evacuate so many

people – that too without
experience?

NIVEDITA GUPTA

So, finally, mission
accomplished.

PRIYA ABRAHAM

Yeh, finally. Thanks,
everyone, and three cheers
for team ICMR!

BALRAM BHARGAVA

This is a very tiny victory.
The real war is still to
come. But this Iran project
taught us another thing, and
that is that you can't win a
war with just two *c*'s. You
need another *c*: courage.

He writes, '3rd C – COURAGE.'

BALRAM BHARGAVA

Now, go home, everyone. Spend
some time with your families
for a change.

NIVEDITA GUPTA

Yeah, for a change.

BALRAM BHARGAVA

I'm sorry did you say
something?

NIVEDITA GUPTA

No, Sir, nothing.

Bhargava leaves. Priya is disappointed.

PRIYA ABRAHAM

People thank cricketers even
when they just draw a match.
They cheer for them. But

no one ever thanks us. No one will thank us for this either.

PRAGYA YADAV

Someone once said a scientist is like a mother of humanity, and a mother's job is the most thankless job on earth, isn't it?

NIVEDITA GUPTA

I would suggest you get used to it, Priya Ma'am.

PRIYA ABRAHAM

Of course, of course, thank us or not we will always keep caring just like a mother.

The remaining people share a moment of silence.

PRIYA ABRAHAM

Ok, girls, good night, and thank you.

She signs off.

Bhargava walks to his desk. On his computer screen is a news report: 'Coronavirus: Can India Survive? - Rohini Singh Dhulia, Daily Wire.' He plays the news.

ROHINI SINGH DHULIA

I am Rohini Singh Dhulia, and I welcome you all to my show. Today, America's Johns Hopkins University has published a report stating that by July 250 to 400 million people in India will be affected by the coronavirus. Four hundred million! Top research agencies from around the world are concerned about India, but our own research agency, the Indian Council of Medical Research, seems to be sleeping because the government is too preoccupied with winning elections rather than focusing on the science. The ones who are truly worried are the common people, who have neither access to medical facilities nor any hope. This is Rohini Singh Dhulia signing off. Goodnight and sleep well.

Bhargava runs out, goes to the control room and looks for Nivedita, but had been gone.

Nivedita shuts her computer and walks out. Bhargava sees her and runs after her to the stairs.

BALRAM BHARGAVA
Nivedita, Where are you going?

NIVEDITA GUPTA
You said go home for a change.

BALRAM BHARGAVA
No, no, I made a mistake, Nivedita. Because of Iran we forgot one thing. Without a diagnosis of this virus, how will we come up with a

solution? We have to isolate
the virus.

NIVEDITA GUPTA
We grow the virus on our own?

BALRAM BHARGAVA
Yes, make a protocol and ask
NIV to start working on it.

NIVEDITA GUPTA
When?

BALRAM BHARGAVA
Now.

NIVEDITA GUPTA
Now, as in, right now?

BALRAM BHARGAVA
Yes.

He starts walking up the stairs, and then turns.

BALRAM BHARGAVA
By the way, who is this
Rohini Singh Dhulia? And the
Daily Wire? Where do these
new sites pop up from every
other day? Just now I heard
her report that by 40 July
crores of people in India
will get COVID, and she gave
Johns Hopkins University
as her source. Anyway, get
going.

Nivedita shakes her head and walks back up. The clock starts ticking.

59 **INT. BSL-4 LAB – DAY** 59

Pragya is briefing her team.

PRAGYA

We will culture the virus samples we have by infecting cells of mice, rabbits and hamsters. As soon as we observe any growth, we will isolate it. This is a very delicate process, and only two or three countries in the world have been able to accomplish it. If we succeed, it will be a massive scientific achievement, and this will be our first step towards saving millions of lives. I am confident that we will be successful in this endeavour. What do you all say?

EVERYONE

Yes, Ma'am, we will.

PRAGYA YADAV

All the best. Let's start.

The pep talk inspires confidence in the gathered female scientists. They all leave the lab with a sense of purpose, including the pregnant Reema.

PRAGYA YADAV

Reema, not you.

REEMA

Ma'am, I can't miss this opportunity.

PRAGYA YADAV

Work from home. It's not safe for you and your child.

REEMA

Ma'am, please, I want to.

PRAGYA YADAV
No. Sorry. Work from home.

Pragya leaves while Reema stands there disappointed and sad.

**60 INT. BSL-4 LAB – NIGHT 60**

Pragya and other scientists begin studying the virus, putting it through various procedures. Cells from mice, rabbits and hamsters are extracted and infected with the virus and the data observed on a screen.

**61 INT. NIVEDITA'S OFFICE – NIGHT 61**

The peon goes past Enna, who is sleeping on a couch, and Nivedita, who is yawning before a computer, when a call comes.

VIKAS GUPTA
Staying over tonight as well?

NIVEDITA GUPTA
What do I do?

VIKAS GUPTA
I understand Nivi, but we have a son too. Just talk to him once. He looks very depressed without you. He is getting nightmares.

NIVEDITA GUPTA
Ok.

Vikas calls out Aditya, who comes and takes the phone.

NIVEDITA GUPTA
What are you doing?

ADITYA
(aloof and distant) Nothing. You?

NIVEDITA GUPTA
We are trying to isolate the coronavirus.

ADITYA
What is 'isolate'?

NIVEDITA GUPTA
It means we're feeding the virus and making it grow.

ADITYA
Isn't he dangerous?

NIVEDITA GUPTA
It's not a 'he'. A virus doesn't have a gender.

ADITYA
So why are you growing it?

NIVEDITA GUPTA
When we grow it in the lab, we understand what kind of a villain it is and what kind of superpowers we need to kill it. Once we understand it's weaknesses, we will be able to kill it just like your Thanos – like this.

She snaps.

ADITYA
But, Mumma, Thanos is very powerful. He killed half the universe. Only the Avengers can kill him.

NIVEDITA GUPTA
So we will have to become the Avengers then.

ADITYA

Mumma, are you never going to come home? Ok, goodnight.

Adity's curtness leaves her wondering. She wakes up Enna, and lies down on the same couch, watching COVID news, in which the American president Trump is heard calling it the Chinese virus and Kung Fu virus.

Just then Ketkar comes in.

KETKAR

Nivedita, do you know this person?

NIVEDITA GUPTA

Ya, China's Batwoman Shi Zengli. She's the director of the Wuhan lab.

KETKAR

Well, this is a fact that this Shi Zengli got the coronavirus to her lab from bats in copper mines.

Then she conducted gain-of-function research on them. Look at this: a research paper was published by Shi in the *Nature* journal 2015 edition. She wrote, 'Creation of a synthetic virus or a self-replicating chimeric virus.' She conducted these trials on monkeys too to simulate how this synthetic virus would affect humans. This means that the virus was made in the lab! Funny, isn't it?

Till yesterday, the whole world was calling this a manufactured virus, but when Trump said it too, everyone went silent. But that doesn't mean—

When he turns to face Nivedita, she was already asleep.

KETKAR
When the truth was standing in front of you, you decided to close your eyes.

He leaves.

62 **INT. NIVEDITA'S OFFICE – NIGHT** 62

The peon wakes up to see Bhargava walking in Nivedita's office. Enna wakes Nivedita up.

NIVEDITA GUPTA
Good morning, Sir.

BALRAM BHARGAVA
Not morning, it's night. What is the update on the isolation process?

NIVEDITA GUPTA
Sir, the BSL-4 lab has tried to culture the cells of mice, rabbits and hamsters but the virus is not growing.

BALRAM BHARGAVA
Enna, I want NIV on a Zoom call.

Enna walks out.

Bhargava goes to the control room as fast as his feet could take him. Nivedita follows, tying her hair.

**63 INT. ICMR CONTROL ROOM – NIGHT 63**

The entire team is on a Zoom call. Everyone is sleepy.

BALRAM BHARGAVA

Priya ji, where is the problem?

PRIYA ABRAHAM

Sir, all our samples are of asymptomatic cases, so they aren't taking the viral load.

BALRAM BHARGAVA

So import them.

PRIYA ABRAHAM

Sir, I've requested all international communities for a sample, but everyone said no.

BALRAM BHARGAVA

Your specifications must have been wrong.

This challenges Priya's scientific competence.

PRIYA ABRAHAM

My specifications? Well, I requested the labs specifically for a SARS-CoV-2 positive specimen having a Ct <30 for the E gene for study. Exact specifications. But they still said no.

BALRAM BHARGAVA

Request WHO.

NIVEDITA GUPTA

Sir, I have spoken to WHO; they also showed their helplessness.

BALRAM BHARGAVA
So should we bow down and give up because WHO is helpless?

KETKAR
I've been saying it for a while. This is a conspiracy. WHO changes their stance every day to protect China. Same with Fauci. CDC is also acting a bit doubtful.

BALRAM BHARGAVA
Dr Ketkar, we will solve these conspiracies later. What I want to know is will we be able to isolate the virus or not?

PRIYA ABRAHAM
Yes, we can, but only if you listen to me.

Bhargava sits down.

PRIYA ABRAHAM
Sir, this virus only remains strong when it is in a living system or at 70 degrees Celsius. If it enters another temperature, the viral load becomes weak. These samples are stored in local labs and then they come to us, but it comes to us at 4 degrees. This is why we're having difficulty in isolating the virus.

BALRAM BHARGAVA
(irritated)
Priya ji, why do you always tell me what the problem is? I want a solution.

PRAGYA YADAV
(from BSL-4 lab)
Sir, Sir, may I suggest? If the virus can reach us before it goes anywhere else, then the viral load will not drop, and we will be able to isolate it before it dies.

BALRAM BHARGAVA
*Ise kehte hain solution.* Nivedita, *abhi isi waqt circular bhejiye.*

Bhargava takes a deep breath and starts leaving. Suddenly, he laughs.

BALRAM BHARGAVA
The irony is the whole world is busy figuring out how to kill this virus, and we are trying to figure out how to keep it alive.

Everyone is amused.

**64 INT. TV NEWS – DAY 64**

ANCHOR ROHIT
Fifteen Italian tourists have been found to be positive in Delhi.

Another person in Noida has tested positive along with his two kids. They were attending a party. The schools of the children have been shut as a precaution.

**65 EXT. PUNE ROAD – MAGIC HOUR 65**

Sanjay drives Pragya. Her phone rings. It's Nivedita.

NIVEDITA GUPTA

Pragya, are you at the lab?

PRAGYA YADAV

No, I left early today. It's our anniversary today.

NIVEDITA GUPTA

Good because today is your lucky day.

PRAGYA YADAV

Why, what happened?

NIVEDITA GUPTA

AIIMS has detected some positive cases, and they have been dispatched for NIV. You must test them immediately.

PRAGYA YADAV

Sanjay, turn around.

NIVEDITA GUPTA

And, Pragya, listen, happy anniversary!

(The clock starts ticking with a monstrous hissing sound.)

**66 EXT. BSL-4 – NIGHT 66**

It's two at night and Sri Laxmi is waiting. A van arrives and a doctor in PPE takes out a sample packed in an ice box. He hands it over to Sri Laxmi, who takes it to the lab.

Pragya opens the box and the isolation process begins.

**67 INT. BSL-4 – DAY/NIGHT 67**

A group of scientists led by Pragya is working in lab as news plays softly in the background.

NEWS

Today, confirmed COVID-19 cases crossed 100,000 globally. WHO issued a statement calling for action to stop, contain, control, delay and reduce the impact of the virus at every opportunity.

A lab technician finds something. He calls out for Pragya.

TECHNICIAN

Ma'am, I can see something. Please come urgently.

Pragya checks the virus through a microscope. She slowly pulls away and starts dancing.

PRAGYA YADAV

Team, we have succeeded in isolating the virus!

Through the glass windows, Sri Laxmi watches Pragya dancing with joy. She smiles.

**68 INT. ICMR CONTROL ROOM – NIGHT 68**
**9 March 2020**

Bhargava walks into the control room. Priya and Nivedita had been waiting on a video conference.

BALRAM BHARGAVA

Yes, Priya ji, what's the problem?

PRIYA ABRAHAM

Sir, there is good news.

BALRAM BHARGAVA
Well, what is it?

PRIYA ABRAHAM
Sir, we have isolated the virus, and with this, India has become the fifth country to have successfully isolated the virus.

Bhargava thinks for a moment.

BALRAM BHARGAVA
Success is not in locating Ravan. Success is killing him. Now you guys think how we should kill this Ravan. If you want, you can rest tonight.

He leaves.

Priya looks dejected. Nivedita too feels it. A quiet sisterhood moment follows.

NIVEDITA GUPTA
Sir is weak in human relations, Priya ji. Thank you and please are not in his dictionary. He's not even expressive, but he's a good man.

PRIYA ABRAHAM
I know. I am sorry.

She wipes her tears.

My family keeps saying that I'm not practical, I'm too emotional and you can tell what I'm feeling.

That's why I left my medical practice and came here on a sabbatical, alone, away from my family. I thought maybe by

working in the government, I
would become more practical,
but I've clearly failed. I'm
sorry. Thank you, Nivedita,
for your kindness.

Bhargava crosses the room and peeps from outside.

BALRAM BHARGAVA

What happened? Why aren't you
leaving?

NIVEDITA

I thought I'd stay. Who knows
when your mood might change.

Bhargava smiles for a change.

BALRAM BHARGAVA

If you happen to talk to the
NIV team, thank them from my
side for doing a good job.

NIVEDITA GUPTA

Sure, Sir. Good night.

Nivedita looks at Priya; Priya smiles at her, wiping her happy tears.

69 **INT. BALRAM BHARGAVA'S HOUSE – NIGHT** 69
**11 MARCH 2020**

Parvati is watching the news on TV.

ANCHOR ROHIT

Today, WHO declared COVID
as a global pandemic. This
pandemic's epicentre is the
city of Wuhan in China.

Parvati switches the channel.

ANCHOR

In America, CDC has imposed restrictions on gatherings of more than fifty people. In New York, all schools have been closed.

Another switch.

RAHUL GANDHI

I will tell you a story. In Andaman and Nicobar, before the tsunami came, the water went out. When the water went out, everybody went to get the fish. When they went, the water levels came up. I have been warning the government. They are fooling around. They are not clear about what to do. Coronavirus is like a tsunami.

Parvati walks out on to the terrace. Bhargava is busy making a bonsai stand erect. She watches him keenly.

PARVATI

Babu ji, are we all going to die?

BALRAM BHARGAVA

Stop listening to this rubbish. Get me a stick.

She brings him a stick with which he makes the bonsai stand.

PARVATI

Did you read this?

BALRAM BHARGAVA

No. Read it out.

PARVATI

The headline says, 'India Can't Do It.'

Parvati goes on to read the news.

'Experts believe that with its population and poor medical infrastructure India will become the epicentre for spreading the disease to rest of the world.'

BALRAM BHARGAVA

Who has written this?

PARVATI

Rohini Singh Dhulia from the Daily Wire. Is everyone in India going to die?

Bhargava is unable to take this but controls himself.

BALRAM BHARGAVA

Have you heard Kabir's poem? 'What you will do tomorrow, do today; what you will do today, do now. There is devastation in the time we waste; what will you do then?' This pandemic is the same devastation that Kabir spoke about.

If we don't take action against it today, it will strike even harder tomorrow. Disasters don't walk into your door; they're invited over.

PARVATI
Babu ji, Kabir wrote the poem saying this is why disasters shouldn't strike, but when a disaster does strike, what should one do?

BALRAM BHARGAVA
Perhaps, Kabir wanted us to write him a few lines.

This leaves Parvati wondering.

70 **EXT. DELHI STREET – DAY** 70

Bhargava is in his car, eyes focused on a newspaper. The headline is Rohini Singh Dhulia report: 'India Can't Do It.' Parvati's voice, 'India can't do it', echoes in his mind.

He looks out of the window, feeling suffocated. He opens the window and inhales deeply. He watches the city pass by.

There are people everywhere. Touching, contacting, coughing, sneezing, spitting. It does seem like a mass grave.

71 **INT. ICMR – DAY** 71
**12 March 2020**

ANCHOR ROHIT
Today, the first death due to corona was recorded in Karnataka, India. The 76-year-old patient had recently returned from Saudi Arabia.

The peon is watching the news on his mobile phone. He sees Bhargava walks in, looking tense. Bhargava notices people everywhere, suffocatingly close to each other. All the visuals are magnified as two sentences echo in his mind.

VARIOUS SOUNDS
India will become the epicentre for spreading the disease to all parts of the world. Corona is like tsunami. Babu ji, are we all going to die? What you will do tomorrow, do today. India can't do it.

**72 INT. DIRECTOR GENERAL'S OFFICE – DAY 72**

Every member of the core team is present: Bhargava, Nivedita, Enna, Panda, Rajnikant, Ketkar, Priya and Pragya.

Bhargava is staring at a newspaper headline: 'India Can't Do It' by Rohini Singh Dhulia.

The team is waiting for him to speak.

BALRAM BHARGAVA
'India Can't Do It.' Why would someone who is not an enemy of India write during a pandemic that India can't do it?

NIVEDITA GUPTA
India is at the greatest risk from its own people. We were the ones behind our 1,000-year enslavement.

PRIYA ABRAHAM
This Rohini Singh Dhulia has been after ICMR from the beginning. I wonder what she has with us.

BALRAM BHARGAVA
Rohini Singh Dhulia is just a face. There are others behind her. But who?

KETKAR
Sir, I cannot stress this anymore. This is a kind of bio-economic war where humans are being infected so that a vaccine can be developed and used to dominate the world's economy. And think about it, if such a vaccine is made, what would its biggest market be? India.

ENNA
Or this virus is being used as a cyber war so that they have full access to our databases with the vaccine? Who knows?

BALRAM BHARGAVA
Just think about it. Why is the media creating such a narrative? 'India will fail ... won't be able to survive ... India can't do it. Who wants forty crore people in India to get infected and why? So that our self-confidence shatters and we stand defeated, humiliated in front of other nations with our hands folded?

PRAGYA YADAV
Sir, you know the pharma lobbies around the world. Who

has bought who isn't really a secret.

BALRAM BHARGAVA

This war is very complex. The enemy is invisible whether it's the virus or the lobbies.

Now is the time to decide whether India will depend on others in this battle or create its own strategy to protect its people with its capabilities. A decision has to be made whether it will be 'India can't do it' or 'India can do it'.

He writes it on a soft board. Silence follows.

BALRAM BHARGAVA

I have decided we will make a vaccine. Our very own Indian vaccine. No matter how much we will have to sacrifice for it. We have already isolated the virus, now let's begin selecting vaccine candidates.

KETKAR

They won't let us make it.

BALRAM BHARGAVA

Who are they?

KETKAR

Superpowers. The ones who have started this bio-war. The vaccine is their monopoly.

BALRAM BHARGAVA

All the more reason to break this monopoly. If this is

a bio-war, then our vaccine should be our weapon of mass destruction. For India to become truly self-reliant, there may not be such an amazing opportunity again.

KETKAR

We're not well equipped for a vaccine. We don't have resources of time. We should focus on an antiviral drug first.

PRAGYA YADAV

China and the US are already working on vaccines. We should also develop our own vaccine.

PRIYA ABRAHAM

I don't agree with you, Pragya. I don't think we should develop a vaccine just because China or other countries are doing it or due to any kind of competition. We should create a vaccine because as scientists it is our national duty to do so.

Everyone shifts focus on Priya.

KETKAR

Vaccine means ten–twelve saal.

PRAGYA YADAV

The actual process of developing a vaccine takes around one and a half years, but the remaining eight to ten years are consumed by permissions, approvals and red tape.

Sometimes it takes an additional two to three years just to publish the results of a trial in journals, if we eliminate the red tape.

KETKAR

Even if we remove the red tape, it's still two years, and that will be too late.

BALRAM BHARGAVA

Why even two years? In a war, why two years? Will we fight the war according to the process, or will we design the process according to the war? Why not by December?

KETKAR

It's impossible.

BALRAM BHARGAVA

In this world, there are two types of people. One who looks at the height of Everest and says that climbing it is impossible, and the other who says, 'Let's at least take the first step'. I am the second type of person. We will make a vaccine, and very fast. The question is, which one?

Corresponding slides are being flashed across the screen.

PRAGYA YADAV
Sir, today, all the viral vaccines in the world or those under development are mRNA vaccines, such as Pfizer's and Moderna's.

PRIYA ABRAHAM
But mRNA vaccines have a problem; they are not as stable as DNA.

PRAGYA YADAV
There are global concerns regarding the safety of DNA vaccines. As of now, approval for DNA vaccines has not been given for use in children.

PRIYA ABRAHAM
What do you think, Sir?

Everyone waits for Bhargava to answer.

BALRAM BHARGAVA
My philosophy is, keep it simple and do what you know best. We should make a killed virus vaccine. Making this will be fast and simple, because we have made these vaccines before.

PRIYA ABRAHAM
Killed virus vaccine is a smart move, and who can be better than Indians in creating the most affordable, beautiful and long-lasting things? We have already isolated the virus; we are

fully ready to start trials
for the vaccine.

PRAGYA YADAV
But don't you think we should
take permissions from the
government?

NIVEDITA GUPTA
I don't see it necessary.
ICMR is a research agency,
and we have a mandate to do
scientific research.

BALRAM BHARGAVA
Until we have complete
confidence that we can develop
the vaccine, this project
should remain among us like
a top secret for national
security. Remember, our motto
is 'under-promise, over-
deliver'.

Everyone agrees.

KETKAR
If we have already decided
to develop the vaccine, then
we should collaborate with
Bharat Biotech. I had a
discussion with Mr Krishna
Ella, and he has also shown
interest in this.

PRIYA ABRAHAM
Why Bharat Biotech?

KETKAR
Bharat Biotech has been in
the game for a long time.
They have provided 123

countries with four billion
vaccine doses.

PRIYA ABRAHAM
Dr Ketkar, if you have spoken
to Krishna Ella, why didn't
you tell us earlier?

KETKAR
Because I still think we
should focus on an antiviral
drug.

Before the argument heats up, Bhargava interjects.

BALRAM BHARGAVA
If this collaboration
happens, it will be a
remarkable government-
industry partnership. Perhaps
the beginning of a new
capable India.

Silence.

BALRAM BHARGAVA
Before you go, look at this
once again. India can't
do it. Write this down
everywhere – in your diaries,
phones, notes, napkins,
bathrooms – wherever you find
a place, because from today
onwards, we have only one
mission.

India *can* do it. In this war,
we have no other option but
to win. If we have to die, we
will die fighting. We will die
becoming self-reliant. Are we
ready for this war?

Everyone bangs the table in agreement.

**73 INT. BSL-4 LAB – NIGHT 73**

Sri Laxmi is inspecting four sealed boxes with details.

PRIYA ABRAHAM
Sir, we are absolutely ready to send four batches of isolated virus for vaccine candidates to Bharat Biotech.

BALRAM BHARGAVA
All immuno-serum, testing system and PCRs?

PRIYA ABRAHAM
Yes, Sir.

BALRAM BHARGAVA
Are they fully secured?

PRAGYA YADAV
Yes, Sir.

BALRAM BHARGAVA
All checks done?

PRAGYA YADAV
Yes, Sir.

BALRAM BHARGAVA
All paperwork ready for the travel?

PRAGYA YADAV
Yes, Sir.

BALRAM BHARGAVA
Ok. Please go ahead. All the best.

In a symbolic act of offering to God, the technicians gathered and break a coconut.

A TECHNICIAN

Ganpati bappa!

All shouts in unison, 'Morya.'

74 **EXT. BSL-4 LAB – NIGHT** 74

**17 March 2020**

ANCHOR ROHIT

Today, twenty-sic countries of the European Union have imposed a ban on all travel.

Four boxes are being transferred to a van heavily guarded by two other vans. The visual is akin to a nuclear bomb being transported.

The van moves from Pune to Hyderabad and offloaded at Bharat Biotech. 'Nasadiya Sukta' plays in the background.

75 **INT. ICMR CONTROL ROOM – DAY** 75

**18 March 2020**

ANCHOR ROHIT

Today, the COVID-related death of the super-spreader Sikh preacher Baldev Singh was reported. After traveling from Italy, Baldev Singh participated in the Holla Mohalla festival at Anandpur Sahib. As a result, forty thousand people have been quarantined in various villages of Punjab.

The peon sees Enna rushing out of the control room. She rushes back with Nivedita. One by one others enter the control room looking worried.

The screen on the wall displays live data of deaths with various visuals. They watch the rising figures with concern.

**76 INT. PMO — DAY 76**

Bhargava walks out of his room, climbs down the stairs and into his car.

He gets down at South Block and is escorted through long corridors and into the PMO.

ANCHOR ROHIT

There is a surge in corona cases in India. Fear prevails throughout the country. The prime minister held a meeting with all the chief ministers. America has suspended all international flights.

The cabinet secretary and few others are waiting. Everyone seems tense. The cabinet secretary takes Bhargava on the side.

CABINET SECRETARY

Are we ready for the PM briefing?

Everyone nods. He takes Bhargava on the side.

CABINET SECRETARY

Dr Bhargava, the PM is not impressed with argons; he wants results. If you want, you can write down suggestions on a piece of paper.

BALRAM BHARGAVA

Sir, I have already.

He shows him a paper.

CABINET SECRETARY

Only two lines?

BALRAM BHARGAVA

Yes.

CABINET SECRETARY
You have a lot of clarity in your mind.

BALRAM BHARGAVA
Yes, Sir; a scientist should have clarity anyway.

**77 INT. DIRECTOR GENERAL'S OFFICE – DAY 77**

Bhargava is searching for something. Finally, Enna helps him find a box of masks. Nivedita, Panda, etc., are waiting anxiously for Bhargava to speak. Nivedita breaks the silence.

NIVEDITA GUPTA
What did you write on that paper, though?

Bhargava wears a mask, picks a paper and gives it to Nivedita.

BALRAM BHARGAVA
Read.

He starts distributing masks to everyone.

NIVEDITA GUPTA
Point one, ban all international flights. Point two, we should impose nationwide lockdown.

PRIYA ABRAHAM
You recommended complete lockdown? Such a big decision. Did anyone oppose?

BALRAM BHARGAVA
There was a very senior officer beside me. Don't ask me his name. He whispered in my ear, 'Dr Bhargava, I have all my relatives in the US.

Please don't stop flights from the US.'

Everyone laughs. Bhargava gets down.

PRIYA ABRAHAM

What was the final decision?

BALRAM BHARGAVA

The prime minister said that only science can win this war. Many people may come to you with potions, remedies and superstitions to cure corona, but all your decisions should be based solely on science. Rely only on science no matter what happens. Don't deviate from it.

NIVEDITA GUPTA

PM actually said that?

He writes on the blank whiteboard.

BALRAM BHARGAVA

Yes, he said, 'Only science must prevail.' Only science.

Bhargava notices Nivedita's eyes welling up.

NIVEDITA GUPTA

Nothing, Sir, just like that. I have been a scientist for twenty-five years. Today, for the first time, it feels like someone is with us.

On the board: 'Only science can win this war.'

**78 EXT. INTERSECTION – EVENING 78**
**22 March 2020**

Pin-drop silence.

The young cop snoozes with earphones on. Suddenly, his dog wakes up and starts barking. He opens his eyes and slowly gets up. There is surprise, awe and wonderment in his eyes. He takes off his earphones.

The sound of thaali banging takes over. People are on their balconies, windows and the streets, banging thaalis for him. It's overlapped with PM's address to the nation about a one-day janta curfew.

79 **INT. DAILY WIRE – NIGHT** 79

Abhinandan, a photographer, is editing janta curfew photos. He turns when he hears a loud voice.

ROHINI SINGH DHULIA

What the hell! Now he is doing politics with COVID also. Frontline workers are dying, and this government is treating science like a toy. Even a child knows that COVID will end through science, not by clapping pans and pots. Not just that. Abhinandan, give me a good photo for this article.

She selects a photo out of the many and goes inside, slamming the door behind her. On the door the nameplate reads: Rohini Singh Dhulia, Science Editor, Daily Wire.

80 **EXT. NIV, PUNE – NIGHT** 80

'Banging Thaalis Will Not Defeat Coronavirus – Rohini Singh Dhulia,' Priya reads the headline amid visuals of the 'thaali ceremony'.

**24 March 2020**

The gardener's son watches the PM's address on TV:

PRIME MINISTER (V.O.)
Everyone should stay where they are. No one should step out of their homes.

Pragya, Nivedita and others are also watching the news.

**81 INT. DAILY WIRE – NIGHT 81**

ROHINI SINGH DHULIA
This is lockdown fascism.

ABHINANDAN
USA, UK, Germany have also imposed a lockdown.

ROHINI SINGH DHULIA
Those governments implemented lockdowns to save people, but this government is using them to cover up their failures. This is a political stunt, but I won't let them succeed in this, whatever it takes.

ABHINANDAN
Whatever it takes?

Abhinandan's and Rohini's eyes lock.

**82 INT. BALRAM BHARGAVA'S HOUSE – DAY 82**

Parvati reads a report to Bhargava:

'1.3 billion people. A 21-day lockdown. Can India survive the coronavirus? - Rohini Singh Dhulia.'

**83 EXT. THE OLD COUPLE'S HOUSE – D/N 83**

The bell rings and the old couple looks through the eyehole. Their faces are covered.

Outside the door, Sanjay waits with some bananas. Packets of milk and newspapers are lying unclaimed at the door.

OLD MAN
Who is it? Arjun?

OLD WOMAN
Don't open the door.

SANJAY
Uncle, I'm Sanjay. If you
need something, let me know,
and keep your windows open.

The old man opens the window slightly with a lot of fear. There is nobody outside.

OLD WOMAN
Don't open the window.

The old man shuts the window.

**84 INT. BALRAM BHARGAVA'S HOUSE – DAY 84**

Parvati runs up to the terrace. The sky is blue, and birds are flying everywhere. She looks down. Emptiness everywhere.

**85 EXT. LOCKDOWN SHOTS – DAY 85**

Various dramatic shots of empty cities with the main characters. In the background Nasadiya Sukta is playing.

CHORUS
सृष्टि से पहले सत नहीं था, असत भी नहीं,
अंतरिक्ष भी नहीं, आकाश भी नहीं था, छिपा था
क्या, कहाँ किसने ढका था, उस पल तो अगम
अतल जल भी कहां था, नही थी मृत्यु जी अमरता
भी नही, नही था दिन, रात भी नही, हवा भी नही,
साँस थी स्वयमेव फिर भी नही था, कोई कुछ भी,
परम तत्त्व से अलग, या परे भी, कर्म बनकर बीज
पहला जो उगा, काम बनकर वो जगा। कवियों,

ज्ञानियों ने जाना, असत और सत का निकट
सम्बन्ध पहचाना, सृष्टि यह बनी कैसे , किससे
आई है कहाँ से... क्या कोई जानता ह, बता
सकता है । देवों को नही ज्ञान, वे आए
सृजन में क्यों? सृष्टि का कौन है कर्ता? कर्ता है या
है विकर्ता? ऊँचे आकाश में रहत, सदा अध्यक्ष
बना रहता, वही सचमुच में जानता, या नहीं भी
जानता, है किसी को नही पता, नही पता, नही है
पता, नही है पता.

(Sṛṣṭi se pahle sat nahin tha, asat bhi nahin, antariksha bhi nahin, aakash bhi nahin tha, chipa tha kya, kahaan kisne dhaka tha, us pal to agam atal jal bhi kahaan tha, nahi thi mrityu, jee amarata bhi nahin, nahi tha din, raat bhi nahin, hawa bhi nahin, saans thi svayameva phir bhi nahin tha, koi kuch bhi, param tattva se alag, ya pare bhi, karma bankar bija pahla jo uga, kaam bankar vo jaga. Kaviya gyanion ne jaana, asat aur sat ka nikat sambandh pahchana, sṛṣṭi yah bani kaise, kisase aayi hai kahaan se... kya koi jaanta hai, bata sakta hai. Devo ko nahin gyan, ve aaye sṛjan mein kyun? Sṛṣṭi ka kaun hai karta? Karta hai ya hai vikarta? Oonche aakash mein raht, sada adhyaksha bana rahta, vahi sachmuch mein jaanta, ya nahin bhi jaanta, hai kisi ko nahi pata, nahi pata, nahi hai pata, nahi hai pata.)

**86 EXT. SOME LABS – DAY 86**

ROHINI SINGH DHULIA

You can see that there are many labs behind me, but all of them are closed. Why? Because ICMR has refused to accredit private labs.

This is happening even during such a pandemic when we

should be granting testing permissions to as many labs as possible.

87 **EXT. NIV, PUNE – DAY** 87

The gardener's son sees Priya rushing out of her house while talking on the phone. She is ranting fast.

He offers her a flower; she takes it but realises it is not safe and asks him to maintain social distance and wear mask. He is confused.

PRIYA ABRAHAM

Sir, don't these dumb journalists know that an RT-PCR lab has to be NABL approved? And they call themselves science journalists!

We haven't said no. All we are saying is that they have to have NABL certification. It's the law.

88 **INT. DIRECTOR GENERAL'S OFFICE – DAY** 88

Bhargava is listening to Priya on his phone's speaker even as he pulls together a long table and some chairs to transform his office into a war room.

PRIYA ABRAHAM

They don't have this much common sense.

PRIYA ABRAHAM

Sometimes I feel like the real pandemic is the media and not the virus. Bloody idiots.

Nivedita enters the DG's office.

BALRAM BHARGAVA
Do you get coconut water in Pune?

NIVEDITA GUPTA
What, Sir?

Nivedita thinks Bhargava is talking to her.

PRIYA ABRAHAM
Yes, Sir.

BALRAM BHARGAVA
Drink that. You will get angry lesser. I had told you there will be a new enemy every day, but that doesn't mean we will fight them all.

PRIYA ABRAHAM
But we need to address this fearmongering, or else it will create panic.

BALRAM BHARGAVA
Ketkar holds press briefings daily. Nivedita, how many private labs have you approved so far?

NIVEDITA GUPTA
One hundred and six, Sir.

BALRAM BHARGAVA
When we announced the lockdown, there was only one lab at NIV. In four days we have one hundred and six. Let them run their mouths; our work will speak.

PRIYA ABRAHAM
But, Sir, the media...

BALRAM BHARGAVA
No means no! We will not talk to the media.

He ends the call.

BALRAM BHARGAVA
From today, this is our war room.

89 **INT. CABINET SECRETARY'S OFFICE – DAY** 89

A high-level meeting is on.

CABINET SECRETARY
What is the status on masks, PPE, Ventilators?

KETKAR
As far as PPE kits are concerned, we produce negligible PPEs, and whatever we had, China exported them all in December because they knew well that this situation was coming.

CABINET SECRETARY
Present status?

KETKAR
We have only 2.75 lakh in reserve.

CABINET SECRETARY
Stop all PPE exports. Masks?

BALRAM BHARGAVA
Sir, the unfortunate thing is that we produce very few N95 masks. We have only 3.35 lakh N95 masks.

CABINET SECRETARY
What? We don't even produce masks? Only 3 lakh masks for

a population of 1.3 billion?
Then import them!

NIVEDITA GUPTA
Sir, we tried to import from China, but they blackmailed us by saying that if we want it by 5 p.m. today, we have to pay many times the market price.

CABINET SECRETARY
Blackmail? No way! This government will do anything, but it will not bow down to anyone's blackmail. What is the solution to this, Bhargava Saheb?

BALRAM BHARGAVA
Sir, we have researched, and India can fight this problem. In villages and the middle class, everyone has a gamcha or a cotton dupatta. If we create layers out of it and wrap it around the face, it can become an alternative to a mask. But the challenge is how to quickly reach this information to every individual in the entire country.

SPECIAL SECRTETARY
Hmmm, I'll talk to the PM. What about ventilators?

BALRAM BHARGAVA
Ventilators are also in short supply. We have only 20,000 ventilators, and since this virus directly affects the lungs, ventilators are the most critical life-saving devices for us.

SPECIAL SECRETARY
The PM has sanctioned almost twenty-five lakh crore rupees.

CABINET SECRETARY
*Bharat ko Atmanirbhar package mein* – whatever you need to source from anywhere, do it. We need to ensure the safety of 1.3 billion people, and for that, ICMR and your scientists should do whatever is necessary. The doors of every ministry are open to help you, including PMO. if you face any difficulties, my phone is open 24/7.

SPECIAL SECRETARY
And wherever flights cannot go, the Ministry of Railways, Ministry of Road Transport and Department of Post can deliver.

NIVEDITA GUPTA
(to the minister of textile)
Sir, the swabs used for testing require Dacron, which is imported, and now that imports are suspended, we have a major crisis.

We have labs and testing kits, but not swabs.

SPECIAL SECRETARY
Such a small item should be produced in India. We will explore the possibilities of manufacturing swabs domestically to address the crisis.

TEXTILE SECRETARY
There is a company that makes earbuds, but they are shut.

CABINET SECRETARY
So open them.

TEXTILE SECREATARY
There is a problem.

CABINET SECRETARY
Don't use the word 'problem' in front of me again.

TEXTILE SECRETARY
Sir, they're a private company.

BALRAM BHARGAVA
Sir, being a private enterprise, there should be no issue. The prime minister's suggestion is to treat this crisis as an opportunity and make India a more entrepreneurial state. When will we get a better chance than this to achieve that?

**90 INT. NIVEDITA'S OFFICE – DAY 90**

On TV, Modi is seen wearing a gamcha as a mask.

SWAB PRODUCER
I have 100 boxes of earbuds. I will send them all to you.

NIVEDITA GUPTA
No. Look, this looks like an earbud, but it is a swab.

Look, its stick should be this big (she demonstrates).

It should have so much flexibility. I have emailed the specifications of the tissue in the swab. I have also sent samples. What should I name the octroi permit?

SWAB PRODUCER

Are you a research agency or a transporter?

NIVEDITA GUPTA

Good question. We are researching on this as well. When I have an answer, I'll let you know.

**91 INT. DAILY WIRE – DAY 91**
**31 March 2020**

ANCHOR ROHIT

Tablighi Jamaat has become a hotspot for corona, and the police have registered a case against Maulana Saad and six other maulanas associated with Tablighi Jamaat for allegedly spreading corona. Due to the apprehension of them trying to leave the country, the Delhi Police has also issued a lookout notice against them. Would it be inappropriate to call this a Tablighi virus or corona jihad?

Rohini walks into a library.

ROHINI SINGH DHULIA

I knew this would happen. The whole world is working on vaccines, and here,

journalists like Rohit
are indulging in Hindu-
Muslim games. Because this
government's focus is not on
finding a cure for COVID but
on finding new Twitter trends
so that people forget the
pain of the lockdown.

She stares at the screen of her phone. On Twitter, #CoronaJihad is trending.

ABHINANDAN
The whole world is
complimenting India's
lockdown, but why are you
targeting it.

ROHINI SINGH DHULIA
Because people tend to forget,
and this government takes
advantage of it by buying
people like Rohit, but I am
a real journalist. I won't
let people forget. That's my
specialisation. Let's record.

Rohini starts to read before a green screen.

ROHINI SINGH DHULIA
The lockdown has ruined the
country more than corona.
Millions of people have lost
their jobs, and businesses
have been destroyed.

Workers are on the streets
with scorching ground beneath
their feet and only the
Almighty above. But this
government is busy dividing
even the Almighty. Our
Almighty, your Almighty.

If it is ours, we will get everything, but if it is yours, you will only get hatred and abuses. Your Almighty is waging various kinds of jihad, while our Almighty is protecting the religion. But the real higher power in India, the one above all, is not revealing how decisions on the lockdown were made. Which expert committee suggested banging pans?

**92 INT. BALRAM BHARGAVA'S HOUSE – NIGHT 92**

ROHINI SINGH DHULIA

The world is busy finding a cure for corona, developing vaccines, but here, we are creating new narratives, searching for new viruses like the Tablighi virus. I've heard that the director general of ICMR is making lists for the higher-ups instead of making what he should – vaccine.

Bhargava and Sunita look at each other until Bhargava breaks the silence by humming, as he smiles, *mohabbat karne waale kam na honge*. (The music picks up.)

**93 INT. BHARAT BIOTECH LAB – DAY 93**
**26 April 2020**

A Bharat Biotech scientist walks into the lab. Other scientists are conducting experiments on mice, rats and rabbits, injecting the virus, monitoring it and analysing reports.

**94 EXT. BHARAT BIOTECH — MORNING 94**

BB SCIENTIST 1

Reports are positive, Sir. It's absolutely safe on mice, rats and rabbits. We are fully ready with three inactivated SARS-CoV-2 vaccine candidates: BBV152A, BBV152B and BBV152C.

BB SENIOR SCIENTIST

It's time to send all the three vaccine candidates for a non-human primate trial to the NIV BSL-4 lab.

**95 EXT. PUNE ROAD — DAY 95**

A Bharat Biotech van is zooming through Pune roads.

**96 INT. BSL-4 LAB — DAY 96**
**6 June 2020**

Pragya looks for Sri Laxmi everywhere, but she is nowhere to be found.

PRAGYA YADAV

Anita, where is Sri Laxmi?

ANITA

Don't know. Anything urgent?

PRAGYA YADAV

Yes.

They finally find her on the stairs talking on the phone.

PRAGYA YADAV
(furious)

Sri, I have been looking for you since when. Bharat Biotech has sent the results that need urgent analysis,

and you are not available on
the phone. How can you just
disappear like this without
informing anyone, especially
during such critical times?

Sri Laxmi cuts the phone.

SRI LAXMI
Sorry, Ma'am, it's my first
anniversary. My husband had
called from Lakshadweep.

PRAGYA YADAV
Lakshadweep?

SRI LAXMI
Ma'am, they are posted there.
They had to leave two days after
our wedding. I was supposed to
join them a week later, but the
lockdown was imposed, and now
this vaccine situation.

PRAGYA YADAV
Haven't you both met since
the wedding? And look, I
haven't even tried to find
out. That's why you're
spending day and night in the
lab. What has happened to me?
How can I be so inhuman?

SRI LAXMI
I understand, Ma'am. Everyone is
under stress, but duty first.

She starts walking back.

PRAGYA YADAV
Happy anniversary, Sri.

SRI LAXMI
Thank you, Ma'am.

Sri Laxmi, Pragya and Anita check the data of the virus candidates that Bharat Biotech sent. Pragya calls up Priya, who is at home trying to find her filter coffee machine.

PRAGYA YADAV

Ma'am, we have analysed all three inactivated vaccine candidates from Bharat Biotech on test animals: BBV152A, BBV152B and BBV152C. All three candidates produced neutralising antibodies when challenged with live virus. Candidate BBV152B produced the highest concentration of neutralising antibodies in rodent animals. The vaccine was evaluated at three antigen concentrations, including two adjuvants.

PRIYA ABRAHAM

Congrats! Pragya, nobody should be able to challenge our science. We need to clear Syrian Hamster protocols because the virus replicates well in upper and lower respiratory tracts.

Priya is making herself coffee.

**97 INT. PANDA'S OFFICE – DAY 97**

Panda walks into his office. Few people are already there waiting for him.

MAN 1

Sir, I have to speak with you urgently.

PANDA

Wear your mask first.

MAN 1
I am.

PANDA
Not on your chin; on your nose!

MAN 1
Sir ji, Sir, I have made an electric bat. Touch to your body, you will feel a current, but you won't die. But the virus will die.

MAN 2
Sir, this is the blood of a crocodile. Drink this and the virus cannot roam around you ever again.

He shows him a bottle. Panda is gobsmacked.

**98 INT. PRIYA'S OFFICE – DAY 98**

MAN 1
Ma'am, hold this pouch like a shield and COVID won't come near you.

MAN 2
This locket will make an ozone in the sky, and the ozone will kill the virus.

PRIYA ABRAHAM
Sorry, what? It will make an ozone?

**99 INT. BSL-4 LAB – NIGHT 99**

SRI LAXMI
(caressing hamsters)
My little baby, are you ready? The outside world

doesn't know that within
this cage, you little souls
are making such a significant
contribution to save
humanity, and that's why I
love you so much my little
darling baby. Let's make a
good vaccine.

Anita observes Sri's behaviour.

**100 INT. NIVEDITA'S OFFICE – NIGHT 100**

Enna is watching videos of people suggesting solutions when her phone rings. A guy is on the other side. She listens for a moment.

ENNA
We have told you your
antiviral has failed.

GUY
Do you know who I am?

ENNA
How does it matter who you
are? It won't change the
report. Please stop wasting
my time.

GUY
What do you think I'm wasting
time? I know everything.
Don't you go home in Noida
every night?

Enna gets scared and starts shivering. She cuts the call. Nivedita notices the change in Enna's face. Enna looks at Nivedita and starts crying.

NIVEDITA GUPTA
Don't worry, you will be
safe.

**101 INT. NIV, PUNE – DAY 101**

Pragya walks with a purpose to Priya's office.

PRAGYA YADAV

Ma'am, there is good news. The hamsters have produced significant amounts of antibodies that neutralised the SARS-CoV-2 virus.

PRIYA ABRAHAM

Has the vaccine cleared the virus from the lower respiratory tract?

PRAGYA YADAV

Yes, Ma'am, and it reduced viral load in upper respiratory tract also.

She shows the results to Priya.

PRIYA ABRAHAM

Looks good! Vaccinated animals' lungs are absolutely undamaged.

Her phone rings, and she asks Varsha to take the call.

PRIYA ABRAHAM

And which of the three candidates is the best?

PRAGYA YADAV

Ma'am, BBV152B is a clear winner. Like a champion.

VARSHA POTDAR

Ma'am, DRDO office.

Watching the test results, Priya asks Varsha to put the call on speaker mode.

SECRETARY

Priya Abraham ji, your scientist Pragya is not approving our antiviral formula.

PRIYA ABRAHAM

Ya, so it must not hold up scientifically.

Pragya wants to say something, but Priya asks her to wait.

SECRETARY

So you won't approve it? Give me your director general's number.

PRIYA ABRAHAM (furious)

Listen, Sir, If my team has scientifically rejected your formula, then I won't approve it either. Even if you want, you can speak to the president or the prime minister about it.

She looks at both Pragya and Varsha, all of them in stunt silence, a moment of bonding.

PRIYA ABRAHAM

I did the right thing, right? Yes, I mean, It's a nuisance. Did you know that India has so much hidden talent? Tell DG sir that if we want to develop a vaccine, then please save us from this antiviral torture. Enough.

PRAGYA YADAV

Ma'am, it's so strange that only science can save us, but the only thing everyone has a problem with is also science.

**102 INT. ICMR CONTROL ROOM – DAY 102**

Enna calls Bhargava, who is walking into the control room. The cabinet secretary is on a video call.

CABINET SECRETARY
Doctor, what does your NIV director think of herself. She rejected DRDO's formula. Fire her now.

BALRAM BHARGAVA
Sorry, Sir, she didn't do anything wrong.

CABINET SECRETARY
Balram, she can't decide what is right for the nation. We have to provide something to the people.

There is so much pressure from all the chief ministers of the states and the public.

BALRAM BHARGAVA
Ok, Sir, shut down science and scientific institutions. Let CMs manage things by consulting with the public. How can I approve something without any data or scientific basis?

CABINET SECRETARY
Can you say this to the PM?

BALRAM BHARGAVA
Sir, I don't need to. He said it himself.

The call ends, and Enna looks visibly pleased with Bhargava standing up for the team.

**103 INT. WAR ROOM – DAY. 103**

Ketkar walks through the corridor with a file.

KETKAR

Dr Bhargava, today is my last day.

BALRAM BHARGAVA

How did I forget! You can't retire, Dr Ketkar. I have approved your one-year extension.

KETKAR

No, Sir, I have decided I want to go. I haven't taken an off for ten years. Since the lockdown, I haven't met my wife even once in Pune. Last month, she fell down and hurt her leg, and I couldn't visit her. Now I want to spend time with her.

BALRAM BHARGAVA

As you wish, Dr Ketkar. You're one of the most senior scientists of India, and ICMR will be forever in debt of your contribution to virology.

KETKAR

All the best to all of you too. But be careful. This vaccine journey is not going to be easy. Till date no one knows where this started. And if the origin is doubtful, how can it have a perfect cure.

BALRAM BHARGAVA
You still have doubts?

KETKAR
Every scientist has doubts, but now people don't ask questions anymore. What is the reason that when this started, every scientist in the world raised academic questions and considered the lab-leak theory to be correct, but gradually, without evidence or answers, everyone went silent? Those who speak, like me, are speaking between closed walls and so no one can hear them speak. Google, YouTube, Twitter, Facebook. If you raise any questions there, you get suspended. Free speech is just a drama. In China, every scientist who raised questions about the Wuhan lab disappeared. WHO, CDC and all the superpowers remained silent. Why?

Why did China's People's Liberation Army's top biochemical weapon expert Chen Wei take control of the Wuhan lab?

Why did a military officer take charge of an academic research lab, and why is everyone silent? Imagine if someone from the military took charge of our Pune's BSL-4 lab.

Were they making a biochemical weapon? Think about it?

BALRAM BHARGAVA

You should rest. We will sit and talk when we have time.

KETKAR

Doctor, I want us to develop the best vaccine, but making a vaccine won't be easy. We may put in our best efforts, but there's a risk that we might not succeed. Even if we do manage to create one, we might not get international approvals. That's why I kept raising questions. But now, it's time for me to turn silent.

He gives him a file titled 'The Vaccine War'.

KETKAR

All my research is in this. WHO will go to China to investigate. If my theory is wrong, burn it, and if I'm right, then—

Enna interrupts the conversation. She had come from the control room.

ENNA

Sir, NIV wants to do a video conference urgently. There is a problem.

BALRAM BHARGAVA

Well played doctor. What conclusion do you think WHO will reach?

KETKAR
Neither this nor that – neti-neti.

BALRAM BHARGAVA
All the best.

Bhargava rushes to the control room. Ketkar is left alone in the room.

KETKAR
All the best.

**104 INT. ICMR CONTROL ROOM – DAY 104**

ON VC:

PRIYA ABRAHAM
Sir, we will have to suspend our non-human primate trials.

BALRAM BHARGAVA
What? How can you even say that?

PRIYA ABRAHAM
Sir, our monkeys aren't the right age, so they are not fit for trials.

NIVEDITA GUPTA
So call from the zoos.

PRIYA ABRAHAM
We need rhesus macaques, and they are not available in any zoos.

NIVEDITA GUPTA
I have an idea. Try tourist spots.

PRAGYA YADAV
We tried temples and tourist spots, but since there are no tourists to give them any food, they have gone back into the forests.

BALRAM BHARGAVA
So go and get them from the jungle!

PRIYA ABRAHAM
How can we, Sir.

BALRAM BHARGAVA
What do you mean?

PRIYA ABRAHAM
I mean we will need a lot of permissions for that. CPC, animal ethics committee, forests...

BALRAM BHARGAVA
So take permissions!

NIVEDITA GUPTA
Sir, these permissions take months.

PRIYA ABRAHAM
If we want to keep the vaccine research going, then we will need permissions at lightning speed.

BALRAM BHARGAVA
How long will you take to get the monkeys from the jungle?

PRIYA ABRAHAM
We just have to go and come, so three to four days.

Bhargava thinks it over for a moment.

BALRAM BHARGAVA
Yes, start working. You have two days.

**105 EXT. PUNE FOREST DIVISION – DAY 105**

A young boy watches as a team of scientists led by a forest ranger navigate a dense forest.

Curious, he follows them. The scientists are not used to such rugged terrain. After a long hike, the ranger stops.

FOREST RANGER
You can get your monkeys here.

The scientists stand there as if frozen.

FOREST RANGER
What happened? Go, catch them.

SCIENTIST
We're scientists. Isn't it your job to catch the monkeys?

FOREST RANGER
No, my job was to find the monkeys. Ya'll didn't get a monkey catcher?

SCIENTIST
Their roza was going on.

FOREST RANGER
So then who will catch them?

YOUNG BOY
You want to catch monkeys?

The young boy emerges from the bush wearing a leaf mask.

YOUNG BOY
The villagers won't let you.

SCIENTIST
Bhau, we are scientists.

The scientist shows his ID card, but the boy can't read. He then hangs it on his neck.

FOREST RANGER
(in local dialect)
This pandemic ... corona ... we are making a vaccine ... medicine.

First, we will give it to monkeys. If they are unaffected, then we will give it to humans. If you help us, we will pay you.

YOUNG BOY
I don't want your money.

FOREST RANGER
So what do you want?

YOUNG BOY
Cure.

SCIENTIST
I promise, I will come back and vaccinate you all on my own.

YOUNG BOY
Will you vaccinate the whole village?

The scientist nods.

When the boy gives a shrill, loud whistle, a few elder kids emerge with monkey nets.

Moments later, they are all seen tracking through a treacherous terrain. The Kids pluck wild leaves as they push ahead.

SCIENTIST
What are they doing?

YOUNG BOY
Plucking leaves to make masks.

The scientist gives him mask.

SCIENTIST

Take this. It's safe.

FOREST RANGER

He doesn't trust this mask.
He only trusts his leaves.

Suddenly, they hear a strange noise from behind the bush. The scientist gets scared, trips and falls over a dead animal before letting out a loud scream.

YOUNG BOY

Shhh, don't scream. You'll scare everyone in the jungle.

FOREST RANGER

No one is scared of anything in the jungle. The only ones who are scared are humans who have captured the jungle.

As the scientist props himself up, his phone falls in a pit.

**106 INT. PRIYA'S OFFICE – DAY 106**

Priya's phone rings. Bhargava is on the line.

BALRAM BHARGAVA

Priya, do you realise it has been eight days, and we haven't got the monkeys yet? Have they gone to catch monkeys or a dinosaur?

PRIYA ABRAHAM

Sir we can't contact the team. It looks like they are in deep region of the forest.

BALRAM BHARGAVA

Do what you must. I am not spending my life waiting for monkeys.

He cuts the call. Priya looks at Varsha.

PRIYA ABRAHAM (annoyed)
I am not delaying it. Should
I become a monkey?

Priya calls the scientist in the forest but is unable to connect.

**107 INT. THE DAILY WIRE OFFICE – DAY 107**

Rohini gets a call from an American man.

ROHINI SINGH DHULIA
What happened?

AMERICAN MAN
Rohini, ICMR has cleared
small animal trials
successfully, and now they
are starting monkey trials.

ROHINI SINGH DHULIA
So?

AMERICAN MAN
So it means they are very
close to making a vaccine.

ROHINI SINGH DHULIA
How do you know?

AMERICAN MAN
The question is how do *you*
not know.

ROHINI SINGH DHULIA
Because no one in this
government talks to
journalists.

AMERICAN MAN
Listen, even if they make
the vaccine, it is going to
be an inferior vaccine. They

won't have the capacity to
vaccinate 1.3 billion people.
The only thing that can save
India is foreign vaccines.

ROHINI SINGH DHULIA
So what do you need me to do?

AMERICAN MAN
You have to create a
narrative that this vaccine
is an inferior vaccine and
make a case for foreign
vaccines. I have mailed you a
toolkit. Everything is there;
just follow it.

Rohini opens the toolkit and goes through it.

**108 EXT. NAGPUR FOREST DIVISION – DAY 108**

The scientists are exhausted from endless tracking and irritated from mosquitoes. The kids know better; they pluck wild leaves and rub them on their feet.

SCIENTIST
What are you doing? You'll
get an allergy.

The young boy says something that everybody misses.

FOREST RANGER
He's saying there is a cure
for everything in the jungle.

As they walk, the scientists step on roots and branches of trees. The kids teach them how not to hurt trees.

By now, food and water are exhausted. The scientists are thirsty and starving, but the kids are practical and resourceful, filtering water from the stream and foraging for food.

They catch a frog and roast it on fire. Another kid catches red ants and makes chutney out of them, and every time they do this, they cry out some vague mantra and perform a ritual, leaving the scientists bewildered.

FOREST RANGER

He is saying to the ants, 'Today, you have helped us; tomorrow, I will help you.' You know, in the language of the tribals, there is no distinction between 'I' and 'you'. There is only one word for both – us – because they believe that when humans, animals, trees, rivers, forests, earth and sky are all one, how can we separate ourselves and talk differently.

The scientists are incapable of eating wild food. They have no stomach for what was being offered. One of them throws up.

After some rest, they walk further. One of the scientists is too exhausted to walk on. The slightest movements and sounds are amplified many times over. He gets disoriented and falls to the ground.

SCIENTIST

Sir, I want to go back.

YOUNG BOY

Till we don't become one with the jungle, we won't find the monkeys.

The boy gives him a locket.

Suddenly, a burly wild monkey jumps over them and comes face-to-face with a junior scientist. The scientist is so terrified that he can't even scream. The monkey stands there staring him right into his eyes.

**109 INT. NIV, PUNE – DAY 109**

Priya's phone rings. The gardener's son is following her even as she receives the call.

PRIYA ABRAHAM
Hello. What? Really? Let me inform DG sir. Thanks a lot.

Priya opens her office and finds two letters, one from PETA and the other from Maneka Gandhi. Attached in Gandhi's letter are a few news reports. She calls for Varsha.

PRIYA ABRAHAM
Where have you been?

VARSHA
A journalist wants to meet you.

PRIYA ABRAHAM
She can go to hell. See this.

Varsha looks at the reports.

PRIYA ABRAHAM
How do Maneka Gandhi and PETA know about our NHP trials?

VARSHA POTDAR
Because Dhulia wrote a story about our trials.

PRIYA ABRAHAM
How does she know?

VARSHA POTDAR
Because we wrote in a science journal that we will be testing on monkeys.

PRIYA ABRAHAM
'We' meaning?

VARSHA POTDAR
Pragya madam.

Priya is furious. She dials Pragya.

PRIYA ABRAHAM
Pragya, did you publish a paper about monkeys?

PRAGYA YADAV
Yes, Madam, in our scientific journal.

PRIYA ABRAHAM
How irresponsible of you!

PRAGYA YADAV
How is it irresponsible, Ma'am. I'm a scientist. if I don't publish my research in science journals, where will I publish them?

PRIYA ABRAHAM
How can you publish without my permission?

PRAGYA YADAV
Ma'am, sorry you are my boss, but I am also the director of the BSL-4 lab. No one has ever asked me to take permissions.

PRIYA ABRAHAM
Well, now I am. Do you know how big of a crisis you have put us in? You have jeopardised our trials. You know how the media is just waiting to pounce on us.

PRAGYA YADAV
Sorry, Ma'am, I can't stop my research in fear of the media.

Priya cuts the phone.

PRIYA ABRAHAM
Oh my God! Now what?

VARSHA POTDAR
We have all the permissions.

PRIYA ABRAHAM
Who did you say is outside?

VARSHA POTDAR
Rohini Singh Dhulia.

Priya decides to confront Rohini. In her hand is Rohini's articles. Varsha is close on her heels. She paces up to the entrance where Rohini is waiting. Priya looks at Rohini. Their eyes are locked.

ROHINI SINGH DHULIA
I'm Rohini Singh Dhulia, science editor of the Daily Wire.

PRIYA ABRAHAM
I know. Why are you here? You know it's not allowed.

ROHINI SINGH DHULIA
Because you don't answer calls and it's a matter of national importance.

PRIYA ABRAHAM
What's your question?

ROHINI SINGH DHULIA
Why are you testing the vaccine on monkeys? You know it is illegal in India.

PRIYA ABRAHAM

No, it was like that before. After COVID, new rules from ICDO came, which made it compulsory to conduct trials on non-human primates. We have all the necessary permissions. Varsha, mail it to her.

ROHINI SINGH DHULIA

When world-class vaccines are being made in foreign countries, then why are we doing this experiment? You know India has never made its own vaccine, that too in a pandemic? All international scientific communities accept that we can't make the vaccine, so why are we doing this?

Priya is speechless. She takes a long pause before taking a long breath.

PRIYA ABRAHAM

Do you even know that we have always been importing technology from foreign countries, and this is the first time in our history that we are doing it ourselves? The hepatitis B vaccine was distributed worldwide in 1982, but it reached India only in 2002, after twenty years. The world got the polio vaccine twenty-two years before us.

It took thirty years for the tetanus vaccine to come to India for mass inoculation. Since independence, the world's pharma lobbies have been arm-twisting and blackmailing us, and we kept letting it happen. Now, for the first time, we are trying to become self-reliant, so why don't you want it to happen?

ROHINI SINGH DHULIA

It's not about me. Why don't we import this technology like we always do? Think about it. For seventy years, why haven't we made our own vaccines? Because we can't. We don't have the capability to make world-class vaccines.

PRIYA ABRAHAM

You are wrong. We always had the capability, but no one ever trusted Indian scientists.

ROHINI SINGH DHULIA

Dr Abraham, please accept it; we need foreign vaccines because we can't do it.

VARSHA POTDAR

Ma'am, DG is calling.

Priya is stressing out.

PRIYA ABRAHAM

Now, if you'll excuse me, I have to get back to work. I

have 1.3 billion lives to
save, including yours.

She turns to walk away.

ROHINI SINGH DHULIA
Ms Abraham, what if you fail?

Priya thinks for a moment.

BALRAM BHARGAVA
How many times have I told
you not to talk to the media?

PRIYA ABRAHAM
But how did you know?

BALRAM BHARGAVA
Don't you know everything is
live nowadays?

PRIYA ABRAHAM
Sir, what do I do? She
entered my office.

BALRAM BHARGAVA
But I told you that you can't
talk to the media means you
can't. How did you go against
my orders?

PRIYA ABRAHAM
Sir, she was spreading
misinformation. I had to
answer back.

BALRAM BHARGAVA
Shut up! Just shut up. We
are not going to talk to the
media no matter what.

PRIYA ABRAHAM
No matter how much they lie?

BALRAM BHARGAVA
Yes! Learn to keep your mouth shut, Dr Abraham. Do not wrestle with a pig because you will both get dirty and the pig likes it. This is not our fight; our fight is only against the virus. If you don't understand it, you can resign.

Anything else?

PRIYA ABRAHAM
Sir, we have got the monkeys. Not one but twenty-eight. They will be at NIV by tomorrow evening.

Bhargava looks at the vaccine trial timeline.

BALRAM BHARGAVA
Start trials immediately.

PRIYA ABRAHAM
Immediately how? First, the monkeys have to be quarantined. Their biochemistry, biometrics and TB testing need to be done. X-rays and ultrasounds will be required, followed by testing their organs for pathogens and conducting bacteria cultures. It will take time. How can it be done immediately?

BALRAM BHARGAVA

These are all delay tactics. When you told me you need permissions in twenty-four hours, I did not ask how? Lightning speed cannot be one sided.

He cuts the call. The gardener's son enters with a flower.

PRIYA ABRAHAM

Oh my God, I can't believe it! We got twenty-eight monkeys, but he has not a word of appreciation. The solution for everything is 'fire Priya' ... 'you resign Priya', but I am not the kind that gives up.

The gardener's son is clueless, but he manages to smile and hands over the flower.

**110 EXT. BSL-4 LAB – MORNING 110**

A monkey handler looks at a monkey.

MONKEY HANDLER

Lord, you have always worked for the welfare of humanity. Now everything is in your hands. If the test on you is successful, then we will all be saved. If there are any mistakes on our part, please forgive us, Lord.

They lift the cages.

**111 INT. BSL-4 LAB – DAY 111**

In the lab Pragya is instructing Sri Laxmi and the team.

PRAGYA YADAV

One team will prepare and collect samples from the monkeys and

another team will immediately
prepare histopathology slides and
tissues. A third team will conduct
serology testing and a fourth team
will perform monoculture testing.
Everyone will work day and night.
Where is Anita?

SRI LAXMI

Her mother-in-law is in the
hospital ... COVID.

**112 INT. BSL-4 LAB – NIGHT 112**

Sri Laxmi is frustrated as experiments are failing. Sri is feeling suffocated in her gear. She runs out of the lab gasping for air. Few scientists are sleeping there.

SCIENTIST

Are you ok?

SRI LAXMI

(in a weird tone)

Yes. Come on, come on, wake
up. No one will sleep more
than two hours.

A monkey is staring at her from inside a cage. She gets psyched but goes close to the monkey, makes a face like a monkey and scares the monkey, and starts laughing.

**113 INT. WAR ROOM – DAY 113**

NIVEDITA

Sir, have you got the news?
Oxford has delivered a 1 ml
vial of vaccine to Serum.

BALRAM BHARGAVA

This is good news. Bharat
Biotech alone may not have
the capacity to provide

vaccines to everyone. And if there is any difficulty or delay in the development of our vaccine, it is essential to have a backup plan.

That's why we need to take two pathways – one with our own vaccine and the other with foreign, promising candidates that will be manufactured in India. Serum Institute is the world's largest vaccine manufacturing company. Even if their vaccine is from abroad, if it is manufactured in our country, it will benefit our people.

Collaborating with Serum is in the best interest of the country. I will talk with Adar Poonawala and tell him if they need any assistance from ICMR, they are welcome.

**114 INT. THE DAILY WIRE OFFICE – NIGHT 114**

Rohini walks into the library. On the news is Baba Ramdev launching his coronavirus medicine.

ROHINI SINGH DHULIA

I have come to know that this government is using scientific bodies like ICMR and NIV for their political agenda.

EDITOR

What is the basis for this allegation, Rohini?

ROHINI SINGH DHULIA
ICMR made a committee two months ago to find out about COVID and its medicines. Today it was shut down, and without a briefing. No one knows why it was shut.

EDITOR
What do you think?

ROHINI SINGH DHULIA
ICMR is failing at making a vaccine. If there is a committee then the people will ask questions. The hard-earned image of the world guru in vaccine development will be shattered. On top of that, there are also the Bihar elections to be dealt with.

EDITOR
What's your plan?

ROHINI SINGH DHULIA
I have planned to do a series of articles on ICMR and their vaccine project. I'll have to see every detail with a microscope – Dr Balram Bhargava, Dr Priya Abraham, Dr Ketkar.

ABHINADNAN
Dr Ketkar has retired.

ROHINI SINGH DHULIA
Oh, I didn't know.

ABHINADNAN
You're a science editor; I thought you must have known.

ROHINI SINGH DHULIA

I want their details. Each and every moment, and for this I need a research team and some funds.

EDITOR

You know the situation is tight. Where can I get the funds?

ROHINI SINGH DHULIA

Please *socho*. People are filled with anger and frustration due to unemployment. They believe that India cannot develop a vaccine, and the image of being the world guru in vaccine development will be exposed one day. And when that happens, where will the vaccines come from? Just think about the huge market India is for foreign vaccines – 1.4 billion people, meaning 2.8 billion doses required. Imagine the numbers. A small share in this market could change our fortunes. If a loophole or mistake is found in ICMR's process, it could mean the end of the world-guru image. This could be a great opportunity to financially revive the Daily Wire and bring down this fascist government.

**115 INT. BSL-4 LAB – NIGHT 115**

Pragya and Sri Laxmi come out of the lab to meet Priya in the corridor.

PRAGYA YADAV
Ma'am, you didn't have to come.

PRIYA ABRAHAM
No, this was rather important. What is the status on the NHP trials?

PRAGYA YADAV
Ma'am, we have administered our vaccine candidate on the monkeys.

PRIYA ABRAHAM
So what's the delay?

PRAGYA YADAV
Ma'am, we are working day and night. People haven't been home for ten days. We are low on staff. Sri Laxmi hasn't slept for thirty hours.

PRIYA ABRAHAM
So? We have the rest of our lives to sleep, don't we? We need to complete our NHP trials immediately!

She walks away.

**116 INT. BSL-4 LAB – NIGHT 116**

Sri Laxmi is watching extremely closely a small copper statue of Shiva oscillating. Her eyes filled with fear.

SRI LAXMI
Create ... destroy ... create ... destroy...

A scientist walks in.

SCIENTIST
Sri, this surgery also failed. Sorry. Here is the report.

Sri is oblivious of her surroundings.

SRI LAXMI
Create ... destroy ... create ... destroy...

Pragya walks in.

PRAGYA YADAV
Sri. Sri. Sri!

Sri snaps out of the trance.

PRAGYA YADAV
What the hell is happening, Sri? Why are we going so slow? I need data faster! Where is the problem?

SRI LAXMI
Ma'am, there is no problem.

PRAGYA YADAV
If there is no problem, then where are the results? I am talking to you, Sri! What is wrong with you?

Sri snaps out of the trance again.

SRI LAXMI
Ma'am, the problem is that the suits we have is designed for 4 bars of pressure, and our atmosphere has a significantly higher negative pressure.

PRAGYA YADAV
Ya, what's new?

SRI LAXMI

What's new are the monkeys we are dealing with. We are testing five monkeys together. First, we need them unconscious, then we have to open them up, then inject them with the virus, and if it works, then we need to take the cells from every organ, harvest those cells and then seal the monkeys.

PRAGYA YADAV

Please don't waste my time by telling me about the process. What is the problem?

Sri Laxmi starts speaking fast in a raised voice.

SRI LAXMI

The problem is that all of this needs to be done within twenty minutes because we cannot administer anaesthesia to the monkeys for more than twenty minutes, and we don't have the expertise to do this all in twenty minutes.

PRAGYA YADAV

But, Sri, you are the best animal laboratory scientist in the country.

SRI LAXMI

No, I am not. I can't do it. I have failed. I have failed you. I have failed NIV. I have failed everyone.

Pragya looks at Sri's meltdown in utter disbelief. She hears a voice.

ANITA
I have a solution, Ma'am.

Pragya looks across the room and sees Anita walk in.

ANITA
For this job, we need a neurosurgeon who can do precision bronchoscopy.

PRAGYA YADAV
Anita, how are you here? Wasn't your mother-in-law in the hospital?

ANITA
She died in the morning.

PRAGYA YADAV
Oh my God, I'm so sorry! Why are you here?

ANITA
Ma'am, we can't go near dead bodies anyway. It's better that I work. This will be the best tribute to her – by making the vaccine.

Sri Laxmi bursts out crying.

SRI LAXMI
What is happening? What are we doing? We are all going to die here, I know it. We are all going to die!

Pragya hugs both of them, Sri howls in fear and Anita holds her tears. Pragya is in a dilemma whether to cry or give them solace like a mother.

PRAGYA YADAV
Have you girls ever wondered why we have so many women in our labs?

Silence.

PRAGYA YADAV
Because we can do it.

**117 INT. PRAGYA'S HOUSE – MORNING 117**

Pragya is washing utensils, and Sanjay is ironing his uniform.

SANJAY
Pragya, didn't I tell you let it be I will do the dishes?

She starts sweeping the kitchen.

SANJAY
Why don't you ever listen?

Frustrated, he looks at their son.

SANJAY
Go snatch it from your mother!

He then turns to his wife.

SANJAY
You only come home for two to three hours, and you come and work here too.

PRAGYA
If you want me to stop, then help me with something.

He waits for her.

PRAGYA
I need your help with the monkey trials. We need an

expert neurosurgeon who can
administer anaesthesia and
complete the process in
twenty minutes.

She looks at him in anticipation.

SANJAY

Hmmm...

He takes a close look at her.

SANJAY

By the way, it's been six
months and you still haven't
worn the lipstick I got for
you. You haven't even touched
the packing of the perfume I
got for you.

She has no answer.

**118 INT. BSL-4 LAB – NIGHT 118**
**26 June 2020**

Sanjay is in the lab helping the team administer anaesthesia to the monkeys.

SANJAY

Twenty minutes is not enough
to do cell culture of the
monkeys. There are four hoses
in BSL-4; we will have to
increase it. Now, let us do
one thing; let us infect them
with a different technique.
We will use intranasal and
intratracheal inoculation
to infect the monkeys. Then
we will put them in the
observation room and collect
results on the first, third,
fifth and seventh days minutely
to see there is no virus.

Finally, when the day of reckoning comes, there is much anticipation in the air. Hearts are beating fast. Tension and suspense fill the room. There's full drama in the lab. Pragya is seen praying.

SRI LAXMI
It looks like the vaccine is working!

A helper walks in.

HELPER
Ma'am, may I—

PRAGYA
What is it?

HELPER
Lord Hanuman's prasad.

He offers chana and gur.

**119 INT. PRIYA'S OFFICE – DAY 119**

A car enters NIV. Pragya emerges from the car and rushes to Priya's room with a laptop in hand.

PRAGYA YADAV
Ma'am, the macaques are showing strong immune responses to the vaccine. The vaccinated groups, unlike subjects in the placebo group, did not develop pneumonia. The vaccine has shown remarkable immunogenicity and protective efficacy. If it is safe in monkeys, it will be safe in humans – 100 per cent.

Our vaccine is almost ready.

Priya is overwhelmed. She takes out some Mysore pak and offers it to Pragya.

PRIYA ABRAHAM
Have it. Mysore pak. Try, you will like it.

Priya watches Pragya eat it.

PRIYA ABRAHAM
Pragya, I am sorry about that day. I mean it.

PRAGYA YADAV
I understand, Ma'am.

PRIYA ABRAHAM
How is your daughter's eye tumour now?

PRAGYA YADAV
Because of the vaccine trials, Sanjay and I had to delay her surgery. But she is very clever. I told her I will come home now and take you for your surgery, and she said, Mumma, come home whenever you want, but don't come without the vaccine.

Priya is overwhelmed with emotion; she holds Pragya's hand.

PRIYA ABRAHAM
Let us inform DG sir.

**120 INT. ICMR CONTROL ROOM – DAY 120**

Nivedita walks into the control room.

PRIYA ABRAHAM
Nivi, finally the vaccine is working!

NIVEDITA GUPTA
Wow! What a good news Dr Priya!

PRIYA ABRAHAM
Where is DG sir?

NIVEDITA GUPTA
He is in AIIMS; he got COVID.

**121 INT. AIIMS – DAY 121**

A young doctor surveys a room full of suffering patients. The sound of the ventilators rends the heart.

Bhargava has a breathing problem. He has a mask on; his eyes are weak. From his room, he can see the suffering of people in the ward. Some are coughing. Some are crying at the loss of a loved one. There are some who are unable to take the bodies home.

A lady patient smiles at Bhargava. She is listening to the song 'Love You Zindagi'. The misery around him breaks his heart. He has not seen anything like it before.

A few doctors in PPE try to cheer up despondent patients. One patient is crying for help but there is nobody to attend to him.

Later, a doctor comes to check Bhargava.

BALRAM BHARGAVA
There are a hundred patients outside, and just two doctors and two nurses.

DOCTOR
What can we do, Sir. About 70 per cent of the staff is down with COVID.

BALRAM BHARGAVA
Why didn't you take precautions?

DOCTOR
Sir, this PPE exhausts you within two hours. We are all working day and night. We don't get time to eat for even five minutes. We don't sleep for two nights at a stretch. The medical staff's immunity is so low that for us to survive would be a miracle.

BALRAM BHARGAVA
When did you go home last?

DOCTOR
Twenty-two days ago. My father had died. COVID. He had a comorbidity. If we had a vaccine, maybe he could have been saved. I couldn't even do his last rites.

BALRAM BHARGAVA
And you're here dancing?

DOCTOR
There is no medicine for corona, so what do we give our patients? The least we can do is make them smile. For all you know that is the real vaccine.

Bhargava looks at the music girl.

DOCTOR
Look at her. She gave birth just a few days ago. She is on the ventilator, but she still has hope. This hope is her vaccine.

BALRAM BHARGAVA
The vaccine will come soon, but don't let this hope fade.

DOCTOR
The vaccine will come when it comes, but I don't know if we will be around to take it.

As the doctor leaves the room, Bhargava lies down, staring at a painting of Krishna and Arjun from the Mahabharata.

Black. Silence.

He wakes up to a deafening silence and sees the music girl dead. Her body is being put in a bag, but her family is not allowed near her.

Suddenly, the sound of crying, ventilators and beeps fill the room. A sense of realisation dawn on Bhargava.

**122 INT. AIIMS – DAY 122**

The DG, Nivedita and Priya are on a Zoom call. Priya notices that the DG is weak but acts determined.

PRIYA ABRAHAM
Sir, how are you feeling?

BALRAM BHARGAVA
Fit enough to fire you.

PRIYA ABRAHAM
Sir, our vaccine candidates are safe on animals. It's time to ask Bharat Biotech to move quickly with the Drugs Controller General of India for permissions to conduct phase 1 and phase 2 human trials.

BALRAM BHARGAVA
Today is 2 July. Can we finish phase 1 trials by 15 August?

NIVEDITA GUPTA
Sir, we haven't even selected the sites yet. To find 100 human candidates, prepare them ... it won't happen so fast. It will take time. It's impossible.

BALRAM BHARGAVA
I have always seen patients from above. The fear of death was in the eyes of the patients, and the hope of living was in the eyes of us doctors. Today, for the first time, I'm a patient, and there was a doctor standing above me, and both me and the doctor had the fear of death in our eyes. Whatever little hope is left will fade, Nivedita, if we do not roll out the vaccine quickly. All agencies should be given a deadline of 15 August.

NIVEDITA GUPTA
Are you sure about 15 August? It's just forty-three days from now.

BALRAM BHARGAVA
Time is for us; we are not for time. Science is for us; we are not for science. If we don't set any deadline, it will never happen. We

will push the short deadline
system, and with the phase
1 vaccination drive, we
can at least protect our
frontline workers and the
elderly population. Draft a
letter and send it to me for
signature. 15 August.

Nivedita compose the letter with 15 August as the deadline and sends it to the group.

123 **INT. ROHINI SINGH'S HOUSE – DAY** 123

Rohini opens her laptop.

ROHINI SINGH DHULIA
Mausi, please make me coffee.

Rohini receives a new email. It's the ICMR email! It has been leaked! She jumps with joy.

ROHINI SINGH DHULIA
Yes! Yes! Yes!

MAID
What happened, Didi?

ROHINI SINGH DHULIA
They are planning on rolling
out the vaccine by 15 August!
But we got them. We got it!
This is the end of the world
guru.

MAID
But isn't it good that the
vaccine will come soon?

Rohini turns to face her.

ROHINI SINGH DHULIA
The vaccine is not coming
soon; it's being rushed

through to coincide with the 15th of August, right? Use your common sense. The reason for this haste is that the world guru wants to deliver a speech from the Red Fort on 15 August. That's why all protocols are being broken.

MAID

Didi, if you don't like the government, why are you taking out your anger on the vaccine? Isn't that for poor people?

ROHINI SINGH DHULIA

Mausi, you haven't understood me still. Have you heard that story? There was a king who couldn't be killed no matter what. Then a wise person discovered that the king's life was stuck in a parrot's neck. He broke the parrot's neck, and the king died. Our king's life is stuck in this vaccine.

The maid looks at her with suspicion.

**124 EXT. AIIMS – DAY. 124**

After being discharged, Bhargava comes out of the hospital and is being hounded by the media. The doctor asks the waiting journalists to maintain distance. He struggles to reach his car. His steps are heavy, and every question feels like a bullet fired at him.

JOURNALIST 1

Was the vaccine programme just a political drama?

JOURNALIST 2

Why is ICMR pushing a substandard vaccine?

JOURNALIST 3

Why are you playing with people's lives?

And then he hears what he had been dreading.

ROHINI SINGH DHULIA

Dr Bhargava, why won't you answer the media? Or do you have no answers?

He pushes through the crowd, ignoring her, but she comes right in front of him and stands, looking in his eyes. Their eyes are locked.

ROHINI SINGH DHULIA

Dr Bhargava, can you please tell me when it was exactly that you went from being a scientist to a puppet of the government?

OLD JOURNALIST

I thought of scientists as gods, always. You broke my faith, you puppet!

Saying this, he spits on Bhargava's shoe. Bhargava stares at his shoe.

**125 INT. THE DAILY WIRE NEWSROOM – EVENING 125**

ROHINI SINGH DHULIA

ICMR and Bharat Biotech have completed animal studies, and now it's time for phase 1 trials in which the vaccine will be tested on humans. ICMR has set a deadline of 15 August, which gives investigators only thirty-eight days to recruit participants and conduct the tests. By 7 July, they need to recruit 375 participants and administer the first dose, followed by a second dose after fourteen days.

Then, a data review is required after twenty days. Thirty-eight days are too little for all these activities. Now, you must decide whether you want to get this vaccine for your children, wives, husbands and old parents in such a rushed manner without any logical reasoning or scientific basis. The only basis one can find is the basis to win the next elections.

**126 INT. BALRAM BHARGAVA'S HOUSE – NIGHT 126**

Bhargava is sitting at the dining table staring at his food. Voices from the day haunt him.

ROHINI SINGH DHULIA

Dr Bhargava, can you please tell me when it was exactly that you went from being a scientist to a puppet of the government?

OLD MAN

You broke my faith, you puppet!

Bhargava feels humiliated. Sunita shuts the TV.

BALRAM BHARGAVA

Let it play.

SUNITA

They're talking rubbish. Please eat.

BALRAM BHARGAVA

I said let it play!

Bhargava is in limbo. Slowly, his eyes well up. It's the pain of an honest man.

PARVATI

Babu ji, last year when I was bullied in school, you told me everyone is afraid of Ravan, but Ravan is terrified of Ram because Ravan knows Ram is correct.

Bhargava is overwhelmed. He looks at her and then at Sunita.

SUNITA

And you are right, so why don't you reply to the media?

BALRAM BHARGAVA

You too?

**127 EXT. DELHI STREET — MORNING 127**

The young cop is walking slowly with the dog. He sees Bhargava's car approaching. As the car pulls over, he notices Bhargava holding up his ID card.

YOUNG COP
Beeroljist, Sir. ICMR? I've heard you are making the vaccine... thank you sir... Please proceed.

Bhargava keeps looking at him as the car drives away.

**128 INT. CABINET SECRETARY'S OFFICE – DAY 128**

BALRAM BHARGAVA
Sir, our internal letter being leaked to the media was wrong. However, our main goal was to streamline the system and motivate people so that red tape can be minimised and trials can proceed more efficiently. I take full responsibility for any impact on the government's image due to this.

He puts a letter on the cabinet secretary's desk.

BALRAM BHARGAVA
This is my resignation letter.

CABINET SECRETARY
You accepted defeat very easily. In the fields of struggle, fighting failure is the biggest challenge. Whatever went wrong, this is the time to fight it not to run from it. Now tell me will this vaccine be made or no?

Bhargava turns the letter and makes three parallel lines.

BALRAM BHARGAVA
It will, Sir. These are the three phases of trials – 1,2 and 3 – followed by manufacturing and distribution, but this will take too long. Instead, if we can do all the three phases parallelly, we can save a lot of time.

CABINET SECRETARY
So what is the problem?

BALRAM BHARGAVA
Phase 1 and 2 we can do together, but phase 3 we cannot until we have the results. We are getting stuck there.

The cabinet secretary walks over to his bookshelf and grabs a book.

CABINET SECRETARY
If your intentions are correct, the universe comes to your aid. Look at this – an article posted by DCGI in 2019, a year before the pandemic, which says during an emergency, a vaccine can be rolled out without phase 3 trials for national interest. Now tell me when this vaccine will be made?

BALRAM BHARGAVA
Sir, very fast. It will be made, first, the most affordable and the safest – the only indigenous vaccine

in the world, India's own
vaccine.

CABINET SECRETARY

So then make it.

BALRAM BHARGAVA

Thank you, Sir.

Bhargava is overrun with emotion.

**129 INT. THE DAILY WIRE OFFICE – DAY 129**
**28 November 2021**

Rohini is watching the news. She opens her laptop and starts typing while the news plays in the background. Abhinandan looks at her disapprovingly.

RAJNIKANT

In both the trials, the vaccine candidate BBV152B induced binding and neutralising antibody responses. The adjuvant in the vaccine worked exactly as we had hoped on the human immune system. The prestigious international peer-reviewed journal *The Lancet Infectious Diseases* has also published our results. Now we are sure: the vaccine is safe and efficacious.

ANCHOR ROHIT

Prime Minister Narendra Modi visited vaccine facilities in Hyderabad, Pune and Ahmedabad today. He said that his government will provide all possible assistance to the

scientists and entrepreneurs
working on the vaccine so
that it can be made available
as soon as possible.

Meanwhile, the Indian Council
of Medical Research has
provided financial assistance
of ten crore rupees to the
Serum Institute and thirty
crore rupees to Bharat
Biotech for vaccine trials.

**130 EXT. ICMR – DAY 130**
**2 January 2020**

Nivedita's car pulls over at ICMR. As she walks in, her phone notification beeps. She opens the news on her phone.

ANCHOR
A very big news is coming in.
Today, the CDSCO has granted
restricted emergency approval to
Covaxin. A new ray of hope has
spread across the entire country.

She jumps and dances in excitement, and when she reaches Bhargava's room, she just stands there in front of him. They don't speak a word. The smiles communicate everything they wish to share.

ANCHOR ROHIT
Let me inform you that
Covaxin will be the world's
first indigenous vaccine made
in a single country.

It has been developed by ICMR
scientists in collaboration
with Bharat Biotech.

Ketkar watches the news at his home with his wife.

ANCHOR
Phase III human clinical trials of Covaxin started in November 2020, in which 26,000 volunteers from twenty-one cities participated.

Pragya, Sri and others celebrate.

ANCHOR ROHIT
This is the largest phase 3 efficacy trial of any vaccine to date. It is being hailed as a victory for Indian scientists who achieved this milestone without seeking assistance from any foreign company, thereby establishing a new chapter in making India self-reliant.

Priya starts dancing. Being too overjoyed, she gives high five to the gardener's son.

PRIYA ABRAHAM
Now the media will be silenced.

She opens the window and takes a long breath.

**131 INT. THE DAILY WIRE OFFICE – NIGHT 131**

Rohini is sitting alone in the office. News of the vaccine rollout is being broadcast on TV.

She searches for the foreign vaccine toolkit and shares it with everyone.

Then she types one article after another while similar tweets targeting Covaxin spread all over the world.

She prints a toolkit copy.

ROHINI SINGH DHULIA
You handle the celebs, you handle the influencers and you handle the politicians.

**132 INT. BALRAM BHARGAVA'S HOUSE – DAY 132**

Bhargava watches the news on his phone. Adar Poonawalla and Krishna Ella are fighting on national TV. He is furious.

BALRAM BHARGAVA
Parvati, do you know how to make a conference call?

PARVATI
Ya.

BALRAM BHARGAVA
Make one for me. Adar Poonawalla and Dr Krishna Ella.

Parvati calls the two men and hands over the phone to Bhargava, who takes it and rushes to another room.

BALRAM BHARGAVA
The whole world is fighting against COVID, and you people are fighting amongst yourselves. The media is instigating you, and you are falling into their trap like children. Does that make you proud? This is the time to work as a team, not to feed your egos. Listen to my words carefully, and there is no argument in this. These vaccines are bigger than me, you or anyone else.

They belong to the people of
India, and only they are the
owners of these vaccines.
You, me and others are just
mediums. Both of you will
sign an MOU right now,
agreeing that from now on
you will never speak a word
against each other in public,
and this MOU should be on my
desk by three o'clock this
evening. Good luck.

Bhargava sits down, tears of anger falling from his eyes. Sunita passes him a tissue.

BALRAM BHARGAVA
Something went into my eye.
Do you have any eye drops?

**133 INT. DIRECTOR GENERAL'S OFFICE – DAY 133**

Nivedita rushes to Bhargava's office.

NIVEDITA GUPTA
Sir, MOU. Serum and Bharat
Biotech have issued a joint
statement that they will
cooperate to ensure smooth
rollout of the vaccines.

Bhargava heaves a sigh of relief.

**134 INT. ICMR CONTROL ROOM – DAY 134**
**16 January 2021**

A syringe plunges into a vile of Covaxin before the needle drives into a human flesh.

ANCHOR
Today, India takes a landmark
step forward in fighting
COVID-19. Today, the first

phase of the world's largest vaccination drive began.

**135 MONTAGE OF VARIOUS SCENES 135**
**20 January 2021**

The Indian government launches a vaccine diplomacy, Vaccine Maitri, to supply the indigenously developed drug to 100 countries.

**136 INT. SERUM INSTITUE OF INDIA – DAY 136**
**21 January 2021**

Adar Poonawala is strategizing with his colleagues on the factory floor.

ADAR POONAWALA
Pull out raw materials from wherever you can. Our new factory is fully ready. By April, we can roll out in full capacity.

The call of sirens stops his speech. A man comes running.

Adar and the team rush out of the factory, and outside, he watches his new factory go up in flames.

CEO
Sir, it seems that changing all the vaccine rollout deadlines will result in a delay of at least four to five months.

ADAR POONAWALA
(whispers)
We can't give up. We have to do it. We just have to do it. The deadline and rollout cannot change. Tell me how to cover up for the time lost.

CEO
But, Sir, if we—

ADAR POONAWALA
(screams)
No sir, no ifs and no buts.
We have to deliver.

**137 INT. TV NEWS – DAY 137**
**26 January 2021**

On TV, farmers are protesting at Red Fort, breaking protocols.

**138 INT. BALRAM BHARGAVA'S HOUSE – NIGHT 138**

Bhargava is peeling kaddu (pumpkin) in the kitchen, and Mukundi is helping him; they are making kaddu ki sabzi.

MUKUNDI
Babu ji, will Parvati be able
to go to study in America now?

BALRAM BHARGAVA
Yes, and she will become a
great scientist in no time.

MUKUNDI
If everything goes well, I will
attend Kumbh Mela this time.

BALRAM BHARGAVA
How come suddenly?

MUKUNDI
When Parvati's mother passed,
I had vowed that when Parvati
passes her school exams, I
will go to Kumbh Mela to
worship our family deity.

BALRAM BHARGAVA
No, no, no; there is a new
strain in the UK. Maharashtra

has reported a few cases. You won't go to the Kumbh.

MUKUNDI

But everything is going well, Sir. Elections are happening, weddings are taking place and markets, flights and trains, all are crowded. After a year, everything seems to be back to normal. I am not the only one going to the Kumbh. Let it be, please?

BALRAM BHARGAVA

I said no. That's it.

Bhargava leaves in frustration, while Parvati looks on.

MUKUNDI

Amma ji, It will be a sin if I don't go.

SUNITA BHARGAVA

Ok, but you cannot take your mask off.

MUKUNDI

Babu ji?

SUNITA BHARGAVA

I'll take care of him.

On TV, visuals of West Bengal elections are playing, making it look like COVID never happened. Protocols are being broken. The peon is watching the news on his phone, coughing incessantly.

ANCHOR

Preparations for Kumbh have begun. COVID protocols will have to be followed.

**139 INT. BALRAM BHARGAVA'S HOUSE – NIGHT 139**

Bhargava is on a video call with Priya.

BALRAM BHARGAVA
Why have our vaccination figures dipped suddenly?

PRIYA ABRAHAM
Sir, people are getting scared of taking the vaccine.

In a village in Barabanki, everyone jumped into the river when health workers came to give the vaccine.

In Kerala, a person climbed the tree. The vice chancellor of Aligarh Muslim University said that sixteen professors have died because they didn't take the vaccine. I have a report over here, Sir, that says globally Indian health workers were the most attacked.

BALRAM BHARGAVA
What is your conclusion?

PRIYA ABRAHAM
Sir, I have fourteen articles here. All written by the Daily Wire. They are all written to spread vaccine hesitancy, all written with malicious intentions, and they are all fake.

BALRAM BHARGAVA
What should be our course of action?

PRIYA ABRAHAM
Expose them, Sir. Do a press conference and expose them.

BALRAM BHARGAVA
No that won't do anything. Your news will be printed on the fifteenth page and that won't stop them. Talk to Bharat Biotech and tell them to do a court case.

PRIYA ABRAHAM
Court case, Sir? Has anyone in India ever won such a case?

BALRAM BHARGAVA
What are courts for?

PRIYA ABRAHAM
I don't know, Sir. This is a media trial. We will have to step out and answer them.

BALRAM BHARGAVA
No, Priya ji, our commitment is with the Constitution, the law of the land. Whatever we do, we will do according to the process.

PRIYA ABRAHAM
Even if they let the people die through unconstitutional and unethical means?

BALRAM BHARGAVA
Let the courts decide that.

PRIYA ABRAHAM
What happened to your focus on the fish eye?

**140 INT. THE DAILY WIRE OFFICE – DAY 140**

The editor walks over to Rohini, holding a bunch of articles. He throws them one by one at her.

EDITOR
This article is yours; this is yours; this, this, this, this are all yours!

ROHINI SINGH DHULIA
Yeah, so?

EDITOR
What is the basis of all this? What is all this? What is wrong with you, Rohini?

ROHINI SINGH DHULIA
What do you mean? I'm just reporting the truth.

EDITOR
Truth? Do you even know that Bharat Biotech has filed a defamation case against us for 100 crore? Are you even aware of that?

ROHINI SINGH DHULIA
What? You must be kidding! These are all facts.

EDITOR
These are not facts. This is targeting.

You're doing a hit job on the government. We criticise the government – that is ok, but if our country is making a vaccine, then what is your problem?

ROHINI SINGH DHULIA

They have made a vaccine, but it is substandard. We don't have the infrastructure to make world-class vaccines. Johns Hopkins wrote about it, and I reported that too.

EDITOR

But they took that down. They said it wasn't theirs. That was fake news.

ROHINI SINGH DHULIA

And how does that make a difference? And chill! Such court cases only have one place.

She tears the notice and throws it in the dustbin.

EDITOR

Rohini, I am against the government, but I am not against the country. I think we need to part ways.

ROHINI SINGH DHULIA

You can't sack me. If I go down, you also go down. Who got all your funding? I did. This office is because of me. Your international network exists because of me.

Alright, you tell me honestly, which vaccine will you take – a tried, tested, reliable foreign vaccine or this substandard Indian vaccine? Who knows if it's just water. Don't look at me like that. Yes, it can be water. You know them—

She walks away as the editor looks at her helplessly. He displays the portrait of a man defeated.

**141 INT. THE DAILY WIRE OFFICE – DAY 141**
**20 March 2021**

ANCHOR
There is a sudden surge in COVID cases in Maharashtra. Experts are saying that a second wave of COVID could hit the country very soon.

This new variant, known as Delta, is being considered more dangerous than before.

Rohini has a smile on her face.

ROHINI SINGH DHULIA
Welcome back.

**142 INT. CABINET SECRETARY'S OFFICE – DAY 142**

BALRAM BHARGAVA
Sir, there is a serious problem. The Biden administration has imposed a ban on providing vaccine resources. Adar has also tweeted to Biden. See this.

CABINET SECRETARY
What about Covaxin?

BALRAM BHARGAVA
Covaxin is self-reliant, so no problems there.

CABINET SECRETARY
This is a new kind of racism – vaccine racism.

BALRAM BHARGAVA
This won't be solved on Adar's level. This will happen diplomatically. But who will talk to Biden?

CABINET SECRETARY
I only know one person – my boss.

ANCHOR
In a major move, PM Modi spoke with POTUS Biden. Later, Ajit Doval spoke with his counterpart, Jack Sullivan.

ANCHOR ROHIT
Today, the Biden administration has given approval to use the banned resources in Covishield after discussinq with India's prime minister. These resources will be sent to India on an urgent basis to ensure that there are no interruptions in the production of Covishield.

Bhargava is watching the news with a sense of satisfaction.

**143 EXT. THE OLD COUPLE'S HOUSE – DAY 143**

Sanjay brings some bananas and knocks on the old couple's door, but nobody opens.

**144 INT. GOVERNMENT HOSPITAL – DAY 144**
**14 April 2021**

ANCHOR ROHIT
Just now news has come that Max Hospital and Moolchand in Delhi have only two hours of oxygen left. The hospital administrations have sought help from the government through tweets.

ROHINI SINGH DHULIA
I am in the general ward of the hospital. You see how people are begging for beds. There is only a few hours' worth of oxygen left here.

**145 INT. BALRAM BHARGAVA'S HOUSE – DAY 145**

Mukundi comes back from the Kumbh Mela. He tries to offer some prasad to Parvati.

BALRAM BHARGAVA
Parvati, don't take that!

MUKUNDI
Babu ji, it's prasad.

BALRAM BHARGAVA
All that will happen later. First, you wait outside. Quarantine outside.

Mukundi let out an outbreak of coughs.

BALRAM BHARGAVA
Parvati, you cannot meet your father for seven days. Keep food outside his room. I will arrange for the RT-PCR test.

In the background, TV news is playing.

ANCHOR
The Maharashtra government has announced a lockdown.

This strong decision has been taken to tackle the rising cases of COVID-19. The Delta variant has caused a lot of loss for the people.

**146 INT. ICMR — DAY 146**

Bhargava walks into ICMR. The first thing he notices is that the peon isn't there. This seldom happens. He looks around for other people.

BALRAM BHARGAVA
Where is everyone else?

RAJNIKANT
Sir, eighteen people in our guest house have tested positive for COVID-19. Hospital beds are not available. In our Gorakhpur centre, forty people have been infected, six of them are in critical condition. There are no beds available anywhere.

BALRAM BHARGAVA
Just because they are infected means what? Everyone else is dead? They won't come to work? Where is my peon, Bahadur? Where is Bahadur?

Panda is quiet.

Just when Bhargava enters his office, his phone rings.

SUNITA
Mukundi's report is here. He is coughing too much. He's not able to breathe.

Bhargava puts on his computer.

BALRAM BHARGAVA
Reports are here. He is positive.

SUNITA
Now what?

BALRAM BHARGAVA
Stay away from him. I will have him admitted.

Bhargava opens a video.

ANCHOR
Delhi's chief minister Arvind Kejriwal said that Delhi is not getting enough oxygen. He urged the government to immediately procure foreign vaccines. The high court told the government to beg, borrow or steal.

147 **EXT. GOVERNMENT HOSPITAL – DAY** 147

Bhargava is in a PPE, trying to admit Mukundi, but there are no beds available.

The condition all around him is pathetic with people panicking and crying for help.

ROHINI SINGH DHULIA
You can see how all around people are lying on the road and footpaths because there are no available beds or even oxygen. Let me introduce you to them. He has been wandering with his elderly parents in a cart for the past four days, but they couldn't find any bed

anywhere. Today, both of them passed away, and now he is taking them to the cremation ground on that very cart.

Bhargava calls someone.

BALRAM BHARGAVA

I need a favour; please arrange for a bed.

He is greeted by silence.

**148 EXT. GOVERNMENT HOSPITAL – DAY 148**

(The young cop's POV.)

Outside the hospital, the young cop witnesses a huge crowd gathering. Eight to ten ambulances are waiting in queue to take bodies that are piling up.

People are fighting with doctors. Amidst the cacophony, a doctor is talking to Bhargava.

DOCTOR

Sir, I have admitted him, but his condition is very bad. You managed to get a ventilator out of turn for me somehow. As long as there is oxygen, there is hope. But please don't have any expectations. I am sorry, Sir.

As Bhargava walks out, a worker affiliated to a political party stops him.

WORKER

You need an oxygen cylinder? Our party volunteers can give it to you. Just post it on Twitter.

BALRAM BHARGAVA
How are you distributing it for free when the government is struggling to acquire any?

The worker disappears in the crowd.

**149 INT. ICMR CONTROL ROOM – NIGHT 149**

Live data on control room screens shows death toll rising. On TV, visuals of chaotic scenes from across the country are streaming. The PM cancels all appointments and addresses the nation.

The ICMR team is watching Rohini report the news.

On the news, bodies of children are being pulled out of a thela and carried to a mass grave – the corpses thrown one on top another.

At another place, fire from funeral pyres lick the oxygen in the air, unaware of the wood shortage nearby.

ROHINI SINGH DHULIA
From what I can see, only pyres after pyres are burning. The lines of bodies seem never-ending. Such a massive failure of the government, but where is the government? Why is no one speaking up? Today, India has become a living and waking funeral ground.

**150 EXT. THE OLD COUPLE'S HOUSE – NIGHT 150**

As usual, Sanjay brings some bananas for the old couple. As usual, he knocks on the door but receive no response. Suddenly, he smells something. Worried, he calls for help.

Soon, an ambulance arrives and the door is broken into. Pragya and Sanjay run up and see the old couple hanging from the ceiling.

**151 EXT. PRIYA'S OFFICE – NIGHT 151**

Priya is on FaceTime with her husband when she hears the siren of an ambulance. She goes to the window and finds the gardener's son being carried away on a stretcher by some paramedics.

He is coughing even as the stretcher is being loaded into the ambulance. He looks at Priya helplessly.

DR ABRAHAM

Are you ok, Priya?

She doesn't say a word. Like the boy, she too feels helpless, breaking down completely.

**152 INT. BALRAM BHARGAVA'S HOUSE – NIGHT 152**

Parvati is crying and pleading.

PARVATI

Babu ji, just let me see him once. I just want to see my father once, please. I won't go near him. Please let me go.

She falls on his feet, literally begging. Sunita looks at Bhargava for an answer, but the latter is in a dilemma.

**153 INT. GOVERNMENT HOSPITAL – NIGHT 153**

An ambulance driver is about to leave, his walkie-talkie crackling with messages. The ambulance is filled to the brim with bodies. Just when he is about to drive off, someone forces a few more dead bodies of young children on the passenger seat.

As he drives off, one of the bodies on the passenger seat tumbles over and falls near his feet. The eyes are open. Panicking, the driver screams, pulls over abruptly and runs out like a mad person. He then goes and crashes onto Bhargava and Paravati, who are walking towards the general ward, falls, gets up and dashes off madly.

DOCTOR

You shouldn't have come, Sir. It's not safe.

BALRAM BHARGAVA

I have to make her meet her father once.

DOCTOR

Sir, that won't be possible. She can only look at him from the outside – ward number 7.

Wrapped in PPE, Bhargava and Parvati walk towards the ward. Parvati is anxious of what is happening around her.

When they reach the ward, they stand there outside and watch through the glass panel.

Inside the ward, Mukundi's ventilator is being removed before transferring his body into a bag. No sooner is his bed vacated, another waiting patient occupies it.

Through the glass panel, Parvati follows Mukundi's body being taken away. His body is flung onto a pile of bodies in a waiting ambulance. Parvati tries to run behind the ambulance, but Bhargava holds her. Suddenly, she goes quiet and becomes numb.

**154 EXT. BALRAM BHARGAVA'S HOUSE – EVENING 154**

Bhargava is lying on the couch, but his eyes are wide open. He hears a haunting melody of '*Raina beeti jaaye*' being played on the flute.

Unable to rest, he gets up, takes the stairs and emerges on the terrace.

There Parvati is playing the flute, covered in snowflakes. The sight overwhelms Bhargava.

He rests his hand on an ash-laden railing. What he saw befuddled him. He steps forward and saw Parvati looking at a mass funeral while playing the flute. In the distance, ash flakes from funeral pyres are drifting about. The ominous sight breaks his heart, and he weeps unconsolably but silently, hiding from Paravati.

But Parvati is aware of his presence. She stops playing the flute and turns back. Their eyes meet. A silent communication takes place.

**155 INT. ROHINI'S HOUSE – DAY. 155**

Rohini is at her desk, going through a bunch of pictures, when her phone rings.

ROHINI SINGH DHULIA

Yes, Abhinandan. See, our photos are selling for 250 dollars and video footages for 400 dollars. Do you want the Ganga ones? They are cheaper. Ok I'm sending you the links. You select and let me know. But the price is non-negotiable.

The maid comes and gets her kaadha.

MAID

Why are you doing this?

ROHINI SINGH DHULIA

Because all this is happening, and it is my job to report what is happening.

She shows the maid few photos on her computer.

MAID

People are also dying in Italy. I have seen how thousands of people are buried together. In America, bodies from the first wave are still stored in trucks. They're rotting there, but you don't report that. And we are selling images of our own brothers' and sisters' funerals to the Americans for a handful of dollars. What are you doing?

ROHINI SINGH DHULIA

This is necessary, Mausi. Till this shock hits the government, they will keep sleeping.

MAID

So you are saying 'India' means the government of India ... the people mean nothing ... the ones who are dying ... their feelings for their families mean nothing? We couldn't give them beds in the hospitals, we couldn't give them oxygen, but can we not let them pass away with dignity?

ROHINI SINGH DHULIA

You think I enjoy doing this? Do I not feel pain? But to make the truth reach the people is my duty.

MAID
The truth? So in your eyes the truth is that only one community is dying .. no one else?

Rohini has nothing to say.

MAID
You abuse the vaccine day and night, but still you were the first in line to take the vaccine. Forgive me, I cannot commit this sin.

The maid walks out of the house.

ROHINI SINGH DHULIA Mausi, how can you just leave? Who will clean my house? Who will make my food?

She's gone, leaving Rohini alone. On her computer the scene of a funeral is playing.

**156 EXT. CABINET SECRETARY'S OFFICE – DAY 156**

South Block.

BALRAM BHARGAVA
Sir, who could have imagined that the wave would come like this. Still, ninety-nine is not a century. We couldn't score that last run because we are always stuck with science. Just this one time, we let go, and we failed.

CABINET SECRETARY
Dr Bhargava, this is a collective failure. But there is a way to salvage this. We have to protect every citizen

from the third wave that
has been predicted to come
at the end of the year. Our
preparedness should be such
that no one can fail even if
they try.

BALRAM BHARGAVA
We will have to change our
thinking. We will need to do
what no one else has ever
done: vaccinate 130 crore
people.

CABINET SECRETARY
We will have to increase our
capacity for that.

BALRAM BHARGAVA
Sir, that will take time. Why
don't we give approvals to
foreign vaccines?

The cabinet secretary walks over to his desk and gets a file.

CABINET SECRETARY
When there was darkness
everywhere during the second
wave, I could only think of
one thing: when everything
in the world perishes, why
hasn't India perished. Maybe
it is because we believe the
universe is one. We never
tried to break or divide
anyone. We believed in us.
This belief is why we have
survived. Now when a lot
of powers want to break
India apart. We have to
decide whether we give in

to blackmail or believe in ourselves and become self-reliant.

He slides the file towards Bhargava. Bhargava flips it open and turns the pages.

CABINET SECRETARY

Now you understand why we did not give approvals to the foreign vaccines? Do what you think is right.

BALRAM BHARGAVA

What is there to think. We have to do what we have to do.

**157 INT. TV NEWS 157**

**21 June 2021**

NEWS: 'Mass vaccination for all above eighteen years of age.'

**158 EXT. DELHI STREETS – DAY 158**

Bhargava is watching the news in the car.

NEWS

The CM of Delhi has asked why the Central government is not giving approval to foreign vaccines.

ANCHOR

Akhilesh Yadav has Tweeted saying he will not take the vaccine. Many others have also said this.

ROHINI SINGH DHULIA

Intellectuals like Anand Sharma and Shashi Tharoor have reminded the people of this country

that the results of phase 3
trials of this vaccine have not
been released yet. Knowing the
results of phase 3 trials is the
fundamental right of a citizen
during a pandemic. After all, why
should anyone take this vaccine?

Prashant Bhushan, a respected
public interest lawyer
of this country, who is
associated with the Supreme
Court, has also stated that
all the judges took the
vaccine, but still, they
got infected with COVID.
You can think for yourself.
If Covaxin is an effective
vaccine, then why hasn't it
received approval from the
WHO so far?

**159 INT. THE DAILY WIRE OFFICE – EVENING 159**

Rohini is in a printing room, watching the news being printed: 'WHO and CDC approve 5 COVID vaccines but not COVAXIN'; 'Why Covaxin is not approved by WHO and CDC?'; 'Why USFDA rejected its emergency use?'; 'Will it affect international travel?'

ROHINI SINGH DHULIA

Wow, wow, wow! Yes!

**160 INT. THE DAILY WIRE OFFICE – DAY 160**

Rohini walks to the editor's cabin with two cups of coffee. She places one on his table.

ROHINI SINGH DHULIA

I have fantastic news.
India's substandard vaccine
did not get international

approvals. Now you know
the power of international
networking. We won the war,
Boss. The government lost.

EDITOR
The government didn't lose;
India lost.

ROHINI SINGH DHULIA
What's the difference between
the two?

EDITOR
That exact difference that we
have forgotten.

She leaves. The editor, a guilty and dejected man, is left alone at his desk. Rohini realises something and enters the room again.

ROHINI SINGH DHULIA
And, Boss, don't forget to burn
the toolkit, and sleep well.

**161 INT. NIVEDITA GUPTA'S HOUSE – NIGHT 161**

Nivedita Gupta's family is watching TV when her car pulls over outside.

ANANT
Mumma is back; Mumma is back.

Nivedita hugs him tightly.

ADITYA
Mumma, I have written a poem
today. You will love it.

NIVEDITA GUPTA
Wow! Let me take a quick
shower.

ADITYA
No, I want you to hear it
first.

NIVEDITA GUPTA

Ok, baba. Ok, my Thor. And where is young Elon Musk?

Aditya runs to get the poem as her phone rings. It's the director general.

NIVEDITA GUPTA

Yes, Sir?

BALRAM BHARGAVA

Where are you?

NIVEDITA GUPTA

I just reached home.

BALRAM BHARGAVA

I am sorry, but please come back. No, it can't wait.

Nivedita starts to leave.

ADITYA

Mumma, please don't go. Please, Mummy, I haven't spoken to you for twenty days, not even a sentence. At least have food with me, please.

He holds her legs and pleads. She pushes him away and runs to her car. Her tears roll down as she drives away.

Aditya sits in a corner with the poem in his hand. Vikas watches as Nivedita's car leaves, then comes and sits next to Aditya.

VIKAS GUPTA

Read it out to me.

Aditya doesn't react; he sits there in deadpan silence.

VIKAS GUPTA
Ok, I will read it.

He takes the paper and reads the poem.

VIKAS GUPTA
Everything is locked up / the sky is turning black—

Aditya snatches the paper and tears it to pieces then runs into his room and locks the door, leaving behind torn pieces of the 'poem' littered in his wake.

**162 INT. ICMR CONTROL ROOM – NIGHT 162**

Nivedita rushes to the control room where everyone is waiting.

BALRAM BHARGAVA
What is the reason? Our data points only in the direction that our vaccine is safe and effective, but WHO is still not giving its approvals. Why?

Everyone is silent.

BALRAM BHARGAVA
Does anyone have an answer or what?

NIVEDITA GUPTA
Let me show you something.

On the monitor screen is a crisp montage of various articles.

NIVEDITA GUPTA
These articles were written one after another. It is as if someone circulated one article, and everyone printed it with different headlines

because people only read headlines, not the main article.

She plays a video showing statements, Tweets, headlines, etc.

ROHINI SINGH DHULIA

Well-known authors and columnists asked why India is not saving its people by allowing foreign vaccines.

NIVEDITA GUPTA

Sir, isn't it strange that all these authors' and columnists' Tweets were posted on the same day with almost the same time gap and in a similar language, as if someone sat them down and gave them a dictation?

BALRAM BHARGAVA

Such lies! How can they spread such lies? That too in reputed international media?

PRIYA ABRAHAM

People think if a science journal has reported, then it must be correct. Then some big influencer quotes them and he posts it. The so-called fact-checkers come and they confirm it. That very day, within a day, the entire ecosystem spreads this lie.

People think when such big names are saying this, it must be true. And without you

even knowing, a lie becomes
the truth.

Sir, we don't address things
to the public, which is why
no one knowns our side.
This is not just a science
war, this is an info-war.
And it can only be won with
information. We should do a
press conference and make out
case strongly.

BALRAM BHARGAVA

No press conference! It is
against my principle.

PRIYA ABRAHAM

This is not a question of
personal principle, Dr
Bhargava. ICMR and NIV have
thousands of scientists. This
is about their reputation
and self-esteem. It is our
duty to step out and fight for
them. This is about India's
people, India's reputation.

BALRAM BHARGAVA

So you guys do a press
conference. I will not talk
to the media.

He walks out silently.

**163 INT. BALRAM BHARGAVA'S HOUSE – DAY 163**

ROHINI SINGH DHULIA

(on TV)

How will the ICMR scientists,
who promoted the unscientific
Covaxin, face the country and
millions of students whose
only mistake was receiving

the substandard Covaxin? And now they won't get a visa to travel to America? Let's see if India's PM, who took Covaxin, will be able to travel internationally.

PARVATI

Amma ji, I'll take admission here somewhere. I don't want to go to the US.

SUNITA BHARGAVA

Don't be a quitter.

PARVATI

I don't want to go to a country that is not accepting our vaccine.

SUNITA BHARGAVA

You know how vicious the pharma lobby is, right? When you're a scientist, you will have to fight these vicious powers. They don't want India to be a vaccine superpower.

PARVATI

So why doesn't anyone say anything?

Bhargava is in his room listening to the conversation.

SUNITA

Because the one who can say something is quiet. You can't be self-reliant by just making a vaccine. You have to defend it too. To step out to fight with a pig, get dirty, but win. That is self-reliance, Balram.

**164 INT. PRESS CONFERENCE – DAY 164**

A sound-guy is fixing cables. The room is buzzing with media personnel.

Panda, Nivedita, Priya and Pragya wait for Bhargava to address the press conference, but he hasn't turned up. As they talk amongst themselves, a journalist asks.

JOURNALIST

More people die in the second wave compared to the first wave even though the vaccine had rolled out during the second wave. Who was sleeping? Were you sleeping or was the government sleeping? Or were both of you sleeping?

PANDA

No one was sleeping. A wave like this that defeated every scientific projection was something that no one had ever imagined. It's the first time in our lifetime that such a thing has happened, and no science, government or society could have prepared for it. But this is not an excuse; it was a collective failure.

JOURNALIST

But there should've been oxygen during COVID. That could have been thought of.

PANDA
India makes a lot of oxygen, but the demand increased fourfold. Who could have predicted that?

RAJNIKANT
The truth is that this has all happened because of the mismanagement of oxygen.

JOURNALIST
You want to blame someone else for your failures?

RAJNIKANT
No. The Supreme Court's audit report states that the Delhi government had exaggerated its oxygen demand by four times its actual requirement. Several political leaders were hoarding oxygen in the name of social service and selling it in black. Oxygen transporters have claimed in the Supreme Court that the Delhi government had no idea how to distribute oxygen.

JOURNALIST
Sir, don't make this failure political.

PANDA
This is not political. Maharashtra also had roughly the same number of cases as Delhi, so why wasn't there a massive oxygen issue there. Is this politics or common sense?

A commotion erupts.

NIVEDITA GUPTA
Listen, everyone, this press conference is about the vaccine, so please ask questions related to the vaccine. The government is there to answer all the other questions.

REPORTER
It's been so long and WHO has still not approved Covaxin. Does this mean that this vaccine has failed internationally?

NIVEDITA GUPTA
Just because WHO has not given approval doesn't mean Covaxin is not effective. WHO has asked for some additional data, which we have provided. It's a matter of time.

ROHINI SINGH DHULIA
Isn't it true that Covaxin was experimented on humans without phase 3 trials? No one knows whether your vaccine is safe or not.

PRIYA ABRAHAM
Your vaccine? I thought it is India's vaccine. Mine and yours. Our vaccine.

ROHINI SINGH DHULIA
Please answer my question. Is your vaccine—

PRIYA ABRAHAM
Once again, India's vaccine.

ROHINI SINGH DHULIA
Whatever, tell me if India's vaccine is safe or not?

PRIYA ABRAHAM
How does it matter what I say because you have already written the headline.

ROHINI SINGH DHULIA
Please don't try those political gimmicks, Ms Abraham. You're a scientist and I am a science reporter. So it will be better if you give me a scientific answer.

A slide lights up the screen.

PRIYA ABRAHAM
Ok, Ms Dhulia, lets talk science. Covaxin is made from a whole-virion inactivated vero cell, which is a tried and tested method. The efficacy of Covaxin against severe diseases is 93.4 per cent and an overall vaccine efficacy of 77.8 per cent against symptomatic infections.

Against asymptomatic COVID-19, the efficacy is 63.6 per cent. The vaccine also conferred 65.2 per cent protection against symptomatic infection with the Delta variant. Now, look at the vaccines that are approved till this date: Pfizer's, Moderna's ya China's CanSinoBIO's. These vaccines that are made with an untested technology, which need to be stored at minus 70 degrees, WHO has approved them, but they are finding it difficult to approve Covaxin, which is based on a proven seventy years technology.

And we are not saying this. This has been published in the world's top-most peer-review journals like the *Lancet*. The same *Lancet* you reference countlessly in your articles. But there are some science reporters who are spreading fake news about our own vaccine without reading any scientific journals. Who is behind them and what is their motive? I don't know, but to think that Covaxin is not safe or not effective is not just illogical but hilarious.

Silence.

ROHINI SINGH DHULIA

Ok, points taken, but please tell me if your vaccine is so safe and effective, then why did you cut short the trial process?

PRIYA ABRAHAM
We did not cut the trial process. We reduced the red tape and approval time, and this is what every other country has done.

JOURNALIST
Whenever you talk about indigenous vaccines, you only talk about Covaxin. But in India, most people have taken Covishield. Why don't you talk about that?

PRAGYA YADAV
Who told you Covishield is not our vaccine? If it wasn't ours, then why did ICMR conduct all its human trials? Why does ICMR financially support Serum Institute? This is discrimination that you are doing. We consider both vaccines as our — India's — vaccines. You focus on Covaxin, that's why there have been so many questions only about Covaxin. For the first time, someone mentioned Covishield too. Why? You know better.

ROHINI SINGH DHULIA
You could not increase your capacity, and you did not allow foreign vaccines to come in. People kept dying. There was a shortage of vaccines, but you kept

sending vaccines abroad through Vaccine Maitri.

NIVEDITA GUPTA
This is incorrect. During Vaccine Maitri, India's requirements were never cut short – only excess supply was sent to needy countries because vasudeva kutumbukum is India's philosophy.

ROHINI SINGH DHULIA
Then why was it stopped?

NIVEDITA GUPTA
No, it was only paused during the second wave because that was an unusual situation. But after the second wave, it was continued, and until October, India provided assistance to all needy countries.

JOURNALIST
Why doesn't anyone know this?

NIVEDITA GUPTA
Because no one in the media ever reported this.

PRIYA ABRAHAM
Because there was no sensationalism in reporting it.

ROHINI SINGH DHULIA
Foreign vaccines kept knocking our doors, but they were not approved, only to prove that by making Covaxin, India has become a self-reliant nation. So that you

can blow the trumpet in the
next election.

NIVEDITA GUPTA
Do you even know why we
didn't approve the foreign
vaccines?

ROHINI SINGH DHULIA
No. Please tell us.

This puts everyone in an awkward situation because they don't know if they should answer it. They discuss amongst themselves.

ROHINI SINGH DHULIA
Please answer. We are
waiting.

Silence.

ROHINI SINGH DHULIA
Shhh, give them a chance to
answer. We are waiting.

BALRAM BHARGAVA (O.S.)
I will answer that.

Bhargava enters.

BALRAM BHARGAVA
I will be answering that.
These foreign vaccines you
keep on talking about – it
is not like we didn't want
to approve them. Their
deal was not in our best
interest. These vaccines
need to be kept in minus 70
degrees before they can be
administered. Do you think
that is possible in India? Dr
Panda would you like to add
some points?

PANDA
Before administering the vaccine, it needs to be taken out from the minus 70-degree freezer and brought to normal temperature. It is initially in a concentrated form and needs to be diluted, but they weren't going to give us the diluent.

BALRAM BHARGAVA
Not just that, you need a special syringe to administer the vaccine, and it is always in short supply. Because of it, a lot of doses were wasted in the US and Japan.

ROHINI SINGH DHULIA
If we talk about our country, it will be better.

BALRAM BHARGAVA
Ok. So there is a rule in our country that if you want to administer your vaccine to our people, you have to test it on our people first, which is the biggest safety precaution. But these foreign vaccines were not ready for this. But you did not raise any questions about it nor did you let this news reach your readers. Why do we call Covishield our vaccine? Because they followed these protocols. Those of you who are advocating for foreign vaccines, let me tell you the

conditions they placed for bringing them to India. We can tell you in an orderly manner. Should I tell you or would you like to tell it yourselves? Dr Nivedita?

NIVEDITA GUPTA

The first condition of the foreign vaccines was that they offered to provide a certain quantity, let's say five crore doses, but they could change the timeline and number of doses anytime as they pleased.

RAJNIKANT

Then, they wanted the Indian government to pay them several hundred crores in advance, but in return, they were not providing any commitment. In case of a dispute, the Indian government had to go to New York and fight the case in the court there.

BALRAM BHARGAVA

The last condition of the foreign vaccine was that they wanted the Indian government to indemnify them against all liabilities, which means that if anyone faced any adverse effects or harm from the vaccine, the foreign vaccine company would not be held responsible, and the Indian government would have to bear all the liabilities. And what was their last condition, Dr Priya?

PRIYA ABRAHAM

It was that if anyone died because of their vaccine, they would not be held responsible. And they wanted this on paper from the government of India.

BALRAM BHARGAVA

Soldiers at the border sacrifice their lives, but they do it for the country. How will you justify the deaths caused by foreign vaccines? We were saved, but there is another country, Brazil, which made a similar deal, and what happened there I think you and your colleagues know better than us. If you don't know, you can go home and Google it.

I am not saying that foreign vaccines are bad, but the question is why you don't consider vaccines made in our country to be good. So let me tell you why. Have you all heard of Thomas Babington Macaulay? He made the education policy of India. He said that if Britain wants to rule over India, then they should fill the minds of Indians with the belief that they are inferior and everything Western is superior.

If ICMR didn't have the word 'Indian' and Bharat Biotech didn't have 'Bharat' but the name of some foreign country, then you wouldn't doubt our vaccine. And that's exactly what Macaulay wanted. Even after Britain left India, Indians remained puppets of his conspiracy, dancing against their own interests against their own country. Now you know who the real puppet is?

Commotion.

BALRAM BHARGAVA

Since the history of this world, not a single day has passed without witnessing a war. Why do wars happen? To conquer someone else's resources.

The world first fought for land, then for wood, coal, iron, copper and every other precious metal.

Then came the age of fighting for oil, and for decades, wars were waged over these resources. But humanity's greed knows no bounds; it said, 'Now I shall conquer space!' And in today's time, there's hardly anything left to claim dominion over. So what do they seek to conquer now? Your mind and your health. This entire data mining phenomenon, these profit-driven social media platforms, they have taken control of your mind.

What we have witnessed in the last two years is a world brought to a standstill, with people wearing masks and confined to their homes. This is about control over our health. I may not know much about world politics, but this is undoubtedly a war against India.

Today, scientific research and development are the world's largest markets, and everyone knows that if India enters the race of R&D, it will be unstoppable because we have no shortage of scientific minds, and that's a well-known fact. Do you know that we didn't even patent our vaccine candidates? Tell them, Priya ji.

PRIYA ABRAHAM

Because patents mean profits. There might not be any country that doesn't patent, but we didn't.

Because we believe that every human has the right to benefit from innovation and knowledge meant for society.

BALRAM BHARGAVA

Perhaps, this is the difference between India and others. This mindset of exploiting profits in the name of health. People want to see India fail in this war.

However, in this war, Covaxin is our greatest victory.

Whether it's in space research, economy or health, it's true that we were once weak, but the same weak child is now standing on its feet and running with the bullies. He may be behind today, but there is every possibility that someday he will forge ahead, and that's why those who are enemies of humanity want to stop us. And by supporting them, you are aiding their cause.

The hall is filled with Rohini's laughter. Seconds later, she claps in sarcasm.

ROHINI SINGH DHULIA

You're targeting the journalist because your logic has failed.

BALRAM BHARGAVA

Journalist? Who is a journalist? A journalist is someone who raises questions. Questions because they seek the truth, not because they don't agree with someone else's truth. Today, when

India is on the verge of victory, you are speaking the language of those who want to bring India down. Why? Is journalism merely about raising questions or is it also about giving answers to those questions once they are found? Is journalism only about accusing people? And when the accused become innocent of those charges, reporting that truth with the same honesty – isn't that journalism?

What kind of journalism is it to defame someone without any evidence? Just hit and run and hit and run? That's what a terrorist does. Your truth is not the truth; it is half-truth, which is even more dangerous than lies. Your facts are not facts, they are selective facts!

ROHINI SINGH DHULIA

How dare you accuse me like that, Dr Bhargava? How dare!

BALRAM BHARGAVA

How dare? Please tell me, when you reported that 400 million people would get infected in India, a few days later when Johns Hopkins gave an official statement that the report was not theirs and their official logo was used illegally, why didn't you inform people about this fact? Because, like an enemy, your work was already done.

ROHINI SINGH DHULIA

You are making these allegations to hide your failures, aren't you?

BALRAM BHARGAVA

Failures? Let's count our failures.

NIVEDITA GUPTA

Our biggest failure is that India developed the world's fastest indigenous vaccine in just seven months.

PANDA

India has also set a world record for the fastest vaccine development approvals through its out-of-the-box thinking and result-oriented approach.

PRAGYA YADAV

Covaxin is the only indigenous vaccine in the world with an efficacy of 81 per cent.

RAJNIKANT

India has administered 100 crore vaccines and is aiming to achieve a target of 200 crore in the next few months. This is the fastest vaccination drive in the world.

PRIYA ABRAHAM
Three times of the US, seven times of Japan, eleven times of Germany, fourteen times of France.

RAJNIKANT
On 17 September 2021, India administered the highest number of vaccines in a single day in the world, providing 2.5 crore doses. This is again a new world record.

NIVEDITA GUPTA
In March 2020, there was only one laboratory in India conducting COVID-19 testing. By the end of the year, the number of labs had increased to 3,390.

PANDA
And yes, in March 2020, there were only 500 oxygen plants in India, and within a span of 112 days, the number increased to 2,500.

PRAGYA YADAV
That's right. During the initial stages of the lockdown, India didn't have PPE kits. However, we became the world's second-largest PPE exporter.

NIVEDITA GUPTA
Same with masks.

PRIYA ABRAHAM

India is the fifth country in the world to have isolated the coronavirus. In the Vande Bharat Mission, we safely brought back one crore eighty-three lakh Indians in two lakh seventeen thousand flights, while many countries had abandoned their own citizens to die there.

NIVEDITA GUPTA

India conducted the fastest and world's largest digital vaccination drive. The CoWIN app has over hundred crore subscribers. Moreover, India provided two-hundred forty million make-in-India vaccines to a hundred countries through the Vaccine Maitri initiative. Most of these countries have expressed that India's help was a godsend to them.

BALRAM BHARGAVA

Your track record proves that your journalism is not in favour of India but standing with its enemies. Not with the truth, but with fake news.

ROHINI SINGH DHULIA

Dr Bhargava, how dare you? How can you accuse me like this? How can you call my journalism fake news? How dare you?

BALRAM BHARGAVA
I do not need to dare or accuse anyone, because today, you are standing in the court of accusations, and it is the court that is saying you create fake news.

A commotion ensued.

BALRAM BHARGAVA
The Telangana High Court has sent a notice a little while back. The court has ordered the removal of fourteen articles written by you on Covaxin, citing them to be fake news, from your websites and has also restrained you from publishing any defamatory articles about Covaxin in the future.

Bhargava reads from the court order.

ROHINI SINGH DHULIA
This is not possible. This is impossible!

The editor stands to join Rohini. There is panic in the hall.

ROHINI SINGH DHULIA
The court never sent a notice. This is a conspiracy. I know you and I know your government.

BALRAM BHARGAVA
Ask the court for your answers. We are scientists. Best of luck, Miss Rohini Singh Dhulia.

Rohini sits down holding her head in utter disbelief.

BALRAM BHARGAVA

In the past two years, I have come to realise one thing – that India is indeed a great country and its people are truly remarkable, especially our women. Perhaps, the world may never fully understand, but you should know that 70 per cent of the women at ICMR and NIV, who are responsible for creating the vaccine inside you, were also doing the dishes, tolerating their husbands' tantrums, taking care of their children and serving their in-laws. When someone got COVID, they were there making kaadha and sending them to help.

Pragya gets emotional.

BALRAM BHARGAVA

When someone cried, they wiped their tears, and they dealt with the anger of mad people like me, but they relentlessly made the vaccine. India is a vaccine superpower today all because of these women. I dedicate this success to all women scientists of India. Now no one can say India can't do it, because India can do it. India can do it.

The surcharged emotion in the room is waiting to burst forth. Just then the editor gets up and claps. Everyone follows. All the women start crying one after another, including Rohini.

EDITOR

Rohini, it is time to accept.

He offers Rohini his hand. She stands up and begins to clap.

**165 INT. ICMR CONTROL ROOM – DAY 165**
**31 October 2021**

Everyone is glued to the TV set.

TV visuals of the prime minister's G20 visit are beaming from across the world. Anchors from International, national and local news organisations are reporting live. It's apparent that the news has taken a life of its own and become huge.

VARIOUS ANCHORS

'Big news is coming from G20 summit in Rome.' 'PM Modi has used vaccine diplomacy and criticised vaccine racism.' 'PM Modi pushes for WHO nod for Covaxin at G20 summit, says India to make five billion shots by 2022 to end vaccine racism where poor and developed nations are deprived of health.'

Everyone at ICMR is watching keenly.

**166 INT. ICMR CONTROL ROOM – DAY 166**
**3 November 2021**

On TV:

ANCHOR
WHO issues emergency use listing for the eighth COVID-19 vaccine. That is India's Covaxin.

**167 INT. PRAGYA'S HOUSE – NIGHT 167**

Sanjay enters in his uniform. Pragya is ironing clothes with her back facing Sanjay.

She turns.

SANJAY
Pragya, now the maid has started coming, and you are still doing the work. Are you addicted?

PRAGYA YADAV
I am. What will you do?

Immediately, he notices a difference. Priya is wearing lipstick, her perfume wafting through the air. Sanjay begins to flirt with her.

SANJAY
I'll do anything, but I won't operate on monkeys again.

**168 INT. A DELHI SCHOOL – DAY 168**

Nivedita and Vikas are at Aditya's school.

PRINCIPAL
I sent him to a counsellor. She says his nightmares and other symptoms are very much like soldiers' families' experiences during war times. I told her, well, after all, he is a soldier's son.

NIVEDITA GUPTA

Thanks. Can you free them early? I want to take them out.

PRINCIPAL

Good luck, Ma'am.

Outside the principal's room, Aditya and Anant are waiting for their mother. She hugs them.

NIVEDITA GUPTA

Come on, my Thor, let's go and have fun.

As the family comes out, many children are waiting for her with flowers in hand. One by one, they offer her the flowers.

CHILDREN

Thank you, Madam, for making our own vaccine.

Nivedita, overcome by emotion, breaks down and hugs the children.

**169 EXT. VELLORE – DAY 169**

Merin and Ananth get married at the church.

Later at the reception, Priya hands over an envelope to the young couple.

PRIYA ABRAHAM

Hotel documents and tickets for Spain. For your honeymoon. A gift from Mummy and Papa.

The parents kiss the newlywed couple.

DR ABRAHAM

Now that we are alone, I thought we should go for a little honeymoon ourselves.

PRIYA ABRAHAM
Stop kidding!

DR ABRAHAM
No, I am serious.

He fishes out an envelope.

DR ABRAHAM
I've bought the tickets. I thought I'll surprise you, but what the hell!

She gets romantic.

PRIYA ABRAHAM
Where are you taking me?

DR ABRAHAM
Iran.

Priya freezes, unable to react.

**170 EXT. ICMR – DAY 170**

Bhargava walks over to Priya and presents her a copy of *Going Viral*.

BALRAM BHARGAVA
Priya ji, this is an advance copy of my book. I got it specially for you.

She is touched by what's written inside the front cover:

'Kudos to you, General'

It's a signed copy.

Priya's eyes begin to well up, but she fights the urge. Neither of them speak a word. Bhargava puts his hand on her shoulder, and they both leave in silence. She clutches on to the book as if it's the biggest award of her life.

171 **EXT. DELHI INTERNATIONAL AIRPORT – DAY** 171
**8 November 2021**

Bhargava is at the airport to see Parvati off.

SECURITY
Passport? Vaccine certificate? Which vaccine did you take?

PARVATI
Covaxin.

Parvati touches Bhargava's feet before hugging him. A pall of gloom overshadows Bhargava's face, but he is happy inside. He lets her go.

SECURITY
If God ever wishes for it, I will have the luck to meet the one who made the vaccine.

Parvati points towards where Bhargava was, but he had disappeared.

He walks out of the airport and disappears amidst a sea of people.

End caption:

'The [vaccine] production capacity of India is the best asset that the world has today.'

—UN Secretary General Antonio Guterres

End visual:

The Indian Science Congress motif with the slogan 'Jai Jawan, Jai Kisan, Jai Vigyan, Jai Anusandhaan'.

The end.

# About the Author

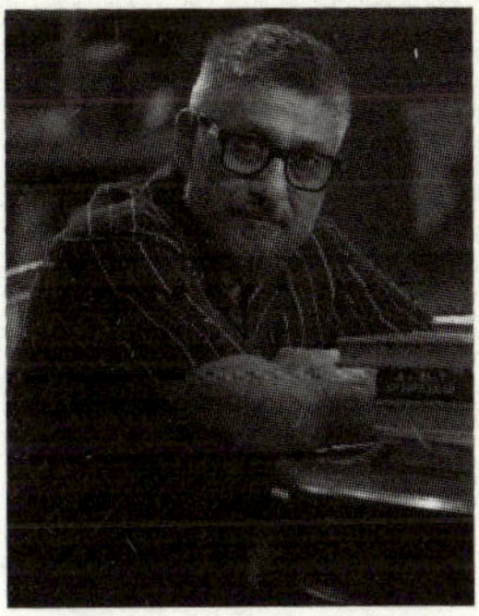

Vivek Ranjan Agnihotri is a national award–winning filmmaker, bestselling author and a freethinker. He was an advertising man before switching gear and becoming a filmmaker. He is popular among the masses and speaks on creative thinking, innovation and various other sociopolitical issues at top global institutes. Vivek is an Indic civilisation crusader and the recipient of several national and international awards.

Vivek's *Buddha in a Traffic Jam* (2016) deals with the contentious theme of urban Naxalism; the film opened with critical reviews but went on to receive a cult following. The first of his 'Files Trilogy', *The Tashkent Files* (2019), became a sleeper hit, wining him the national award for best screenplay/dialogues. The second, *The Kashmir Files* (2022), disrupted the market by becoming an all-time blockbuster at the box office and collecting the Nargis Dutt Award for Best Feature Film on National Integration at the 69th National Film Awards. His latest, *The Vaccine War*, India's first bioscience film, hit theatres in September 2023, garnering exceptional response from the audience as well as critical acclaim. The script has been officially selected by the Margaret Herrick Library of the Academy of Motion Picture Arts and Sciences, which awards Oscars. It was also selected for screening in the Indian Panorama section of the 54th International Film Festival of India.

Vivek's debut book, *Urban Naxals*, became the fastest-selling #1 bestseller. His other books include the historical nonfiction

*Who Killed Shastri? The Tashkent Files* and the philosophical *The Book of Life: My Dance with Buddha for Success.*

He is married to the national award-winning actor Pallavi Joshi. They run an NGO, I Am Buddha Foundation, which mentors and trains disadvantaged youth in creative thinking. They have two children.